Julius Nyerere

OHIO SHORT HISTORIES OF AFRICA

This series of Ohio Short Histories of Africa is meant for those who are looking for a brief but lively introduction to a wide range of topics in African history, politics, and biography, written by some of the leading experts in their fields.

Julius Nyerere

Paul Bjerk

OHIO UNIVERSITY PRESS

ATHENS

Ohio University Press, Athens, Ohio 45701
ohioswallow.com
© 2017 by Ohio University Press
All rights reserved

Printed in the United States of America
Ohio University Press books are printed on acid-free paper ♾ ™

27 26 25 24 23 22 21 20 19 18 17   5 4 3 2 1

Cover design by Joey Hi-Fi

Library of Congress Cataloging-in-Publication Data
Names: Bjerk, Paul, author.
Title: Julius Nyerere / Paul Bjerk.
Other titles: Ohio short histories of Africa.
Description: Athens, Ohio : Ohio University Press, 2017. | Series:
Ohio short
  histories of Africa | Includes bibliographical references and index.
Identifiers: LCCN 2017004209| ISBN 9780821422601 (pb : alk. pa-
per) | ISBN
  9780821445969 (pdf)
Subjects: LCSH: Nyerere, Julius K., 1922–1999. |
  Presidents—Tanzania—Biography. | Nation-building—Tanzania. |
  Tanzania—History—20th century. | Tanzania—Politics and govern-
ment—20th
  century.
Classification: LCC DT448.25.N9 B542 2017 | DDC 967.8041092—
dc23
LC record available at https://lccn.loc.gov/2017004209

Contents

Illustrations

Figures

Map

1

Mwalimu Nyerere

A Study in Leadership

In January 2006 a delegation from the Vatican held a mass in the Tanzanian village of Butiama to begin investigating the life of Julius Kambarage Nyerere for beatification.[1] This is usually the first step toward sainthood. But it is an unusual honor for a socialist dictator.

Neither saint nor tyrant, Nyerere was a politician who kept his integrity and vision in a harsh and changing world. He taught high school upon graduating from college in 1943, and for the rest of his life he was happiest to be called *Mwalimu*, the Swahili word for "teacher." He became the first prime minister of independent Tanganyika in 1961, its first president in 1962, and brokered a merger with Zanzibar to become Tanzania in 1964. Prior to the presidency he headed a mass movement that skillfully brought Tanganyika to independence without violence. He was an advocate for democracy, but by reasoning that each country built its own style of democracy, he built a one-party state that regularly violated democratic values.

Nyerere pursued ambitious and not always successful policies aimed at building a peaceful and prosperous nation out of an ethnically diverse colonial territory populated mostly by illiterate peasant farmers. His Arusha Declaration in 1967 envisioned a clean government dedicated to economic growth on the basis of his theory of African socialism, or *Ujamaa*. Although his government gave military support to movements fighting white-minority governments, only the war with Idi Amin's Uganda in 1978 mobilized the Tanzanian army and population at large. From his retirement in 1985 to his death in 1999, he used his prestige to urge for ethical political choices at home and abroad. Everyone who met him regarded him as a brilliant intellectual, but some of his policies seem disastrously misguided to us today.

As we are apt to do with historical figures, we lay claim to Julius Nyerere as a symbol of our aspirations and our nightmares; of our heroes and our villains. Yet a full-length, researched biography has not yet been written. In this sketch of his life, I seek to claim him instead as a symbol of leadership and its perils. There will be much debate before a scholarly, let alone popular, consensus is formed around these events. My hope is that this portrait can serve as a case study of an African country confronting the challenges of independence, as seen through the life of one of the era's most creative and thoughtful politicians.

Nyerere laid out an intellectual and political project and then took deliberate steps to organize people in pursuit of that project. He saw decolonization as an opportunity to build a new society: "The Africa that we must create . . . cannot be an Africa which is simply free from foreign domination. It must be an Africa which the outside world will look at and say: 'Here is a continent which has truly free human beings. . . . That is the continent of hope for the human race.'"[2]

His life and leadership encompassed the contradictions of his age, and those contradictions beguile us long after his death. While the Vatican may eventually find its own grounds for honoring Nyerere, such veneration is highly politicized and robs history of its human reality, where lessons might be learned from both success and failure. With a stubborn streak that easily blocked common sense, he was far from perfect. But by the same token, those who count Nyerere as a villain pursuing a "systematic campaign to deny [Muslims] basic rights," as Aboud Jumbe resentfully put it, only set him up as a scapegoat for more complex social trends.[3]

Few leaders so assiduously cultivated an inclusive political establishment or so vehemently denounced the prejudices of their own societies. Nyerere made sure his government and his closest associates reflected a cross-section of Tanzania's diverse society—Muslim, Christian, Hindu, and animist; African, Indian, Arab, and European—inclusive of all the countless ethnic groups of its broad territory. While those who suffered from his economic policies and political repression may cast him in the role of a Third World strongman, any honest account must also acknowledge his humility, his

Figure 1.1 The independence cabinet, 1961. *Rear, from left:* Minister of Local Government Job Lusinde; Minister without Portfolio Rashidi Kawawa; Minister of Commerce and Industry Nsilo Swai; Minister of Education Oscar Kambona; Minister of Lands, Forests, and Wildlife Tewa Saidi Tewa; Cabinet Secretary Charles Meek. *Front, from left:* Minister of Agriculture Paul Bomani; Minister of Legal Affairs Abdallah Fundikira; Prime Minister Julius Nyerere; Minister of Finance Ernest Vasey; Minister of Communications, Power, and Works Amir Jamal. *Not pictured:* Minister of Home Affairs George Kahama and Minister of Health and Labour Derek Bryceson. © Tanzania Information Services/MAELEZO.

restraint, and his real commitment to a better life for the people of his country.

Late in life he offered lessons on leadership as the country prepared for its first multiparty presidential elections since independence. "A president of our country is chosen based on the constitution of Tanzania. And, upon being chosen, the person is sworn in: if a Christian, upon the Bible; if a Muslim, upon the Koran. We have not yet chosen a candidate who doesn't believe in God, but when we do, we'll find some way to swear the chap in!"[4] He insisted that

> a President must be able to lead the country. He is
> not there simply to execute popular demands if he
> recognises or believes that the consequences could
> be disastrous for the people or for the independence
> of the country. Yet he is responsible to the People;
> he needs their confidence and support. . . . [The
> President] needs to be a person of complete honesty
> and integrity, capable, strong, firm, and with clear
> principles which he can explain and defend.[5]

This was not mere rhetoric. This was the standard to which he held himself. "A President's decisions are almost always difficult—easier ones can be made by his Ministers or Officials. And failure to decide is itself a decision: quite frequently refusing (or being unable) to make a decision is worse than making the one which time will prove to have been wrong! For the absence of any decision leads to confusion and opens the door to exploitation by crooks." Nyerere had a scholar's mind, but did not have the luxury to wrestle with ideas in the abstract. A politician's ideas affect people's lives. "To plan means to choose," is the way Nyerere described the challenge of governance at the height of his presidency, and after his retirement he noted that he did not always make perfect choices.[6]

Whether in the fight to wrest a colony away from the clutches of an imperial power or the fight to guide the direction of an independent country, politics entails the competition for power. Political systems are designed to manage and contain the conflict inherent in this struggle. But systems fail, and politics can easily turn violent. Newly established political systems are especially prone to violence where there is little consensus over rules and norms, where there is little respect for the rights of those who don't wield power, where there is little faith that those out of office will ever peacefully come into office. Peaceful politics requires compromise, tolerance, and benevolence.

Nyerere engaged in this competition for power in order to establish a peaceful political system. He trusted his vision and considered his leadership essential to establishing such a system. His tools were his ability with words and his management of political institutions. He knew that success would entail a system that could function without him and he made it his goal to step down from power of his own accord. Establishing such a system during his time in office, however, required power, and power is difficult for anyone to manage. By the 1970s, Nyerere was overseeing a creeping police state, administered by officials whose habits even he could not fully control.

His peers, the presidents and prime ministers of the newly independent countries of Africa, faced the same challenge. All of them sought power. All of them had visions, some more selfish than others. All of them faced challenges and opposition. In basic ways, Nyerere was like his peers. Most of them were only a generation re-moved from a village society of hand tools and family authorities. They were among the first from their colo-nized peoples to receive a European education. They saw their task as one of combining the best of their African cultural roots with those aspects of the coloniz-er's culture that could benefit African society.[7]

Given the life-changing difficulty of this task, the competition and temptations of power and global po-litical realities, leadership in postcolonial Africa was a perilous responsibility. Leaders held on to power by intimidating, often eliminating, those who would question them, by controlling the distribution of the nation's wealth, and by setting segments of society in conflict with each other. A number of his peers were overthrown, sent into exile, or assassinated. Nyerere survived to step down of his own accord and live out his life as an active citizen of his home country. Such an accomplishment in the context of postcolonial Africa was never a saintly one.

Historical and Political Context

In the 1800s, as Britain led the effort to end the Atlantic slave trade, trade in slaves across the Indian Ocean grew and extended across East Africa. Where the Atlantic slave trade had been dominated and justified by Christian capitalists, the Indian Ocean slave trade was dominated by Muslim traders with roots in Africa and the Mid-dle East. From the mid-1800s, increasingly aggressive

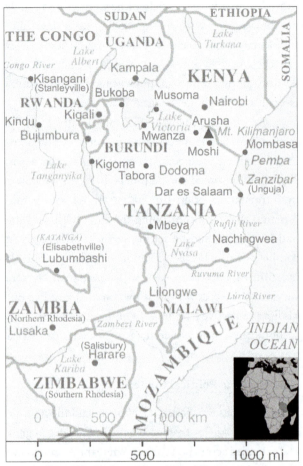

Map 1.1 East Africa. Adapted from United Nations Department of Peacekeeping Operations. © United Nations.

strategies to capture slaves and ivory brought violence and disruption to farming societies, among whom the benefits of trade had traditionally outweighed costs of conflict. Seeking protection, villagers submitted to war-lords like Tippu Tip, the slave trader and clove planter whose political influence stretched from Zanzibar to the Congo River, or warrior kings like the Hehe leaders in Iringa, Muyigumba and his son Mkwawa, who built up standing armies with taxes levied on conquered peoples.

The interior was a diverse place harboring both hierarchical and decentralized societies as well as scores of distinct languages and cultural traditions. In political and economic terms, the export of slaves—as well as ivory, decorative woods, and cloves—meant that the coast and the interior became linked more intimately than they had been in the past. Not only did Islamic culture spread inland, but also the coastal Swahili language, with its heavy load of Arabic vocabulary superimposed on an African grammar.[8]

Toward the end of the century, European countries entered a heated global competition for colonies, and the antislavery cause gave them a convenient justification for seeking influence in Africa. In East Africa, a mission-ary named David Livingstone witnessed the devastation caused by the slave trade and advocated the antislavery movement's concept of "commerce, Christianity, and civilization" as a means to its end. He was the first of many missionaries who followed the paths of Muslim caravan traders to establish Christian communities throughout the region.[9] The early missionaries met with little success at first. Following in their path, however, were businessmen and soldiers who colonized Africa for European settlement and the production of raw materials in high demand because of industrialization in Europe.

By the mid-1900s, a generation had grown up under colonial rule in Africa. Some had witnessed aspects of the devastating European wars, others became familiar with European practices of business and governance, and a precious few gained a European education. In East Africa, the British had welcomed immigration from India because the immigrants could help administer colonial rule and expand commercial trade across the territory. European rule became a familiar presence, bringing significant benefits and a host of new problems. People resented the racial hierarchy that came with it, which set aside innumerable privileges for Europeans, offered Indian immigrants favorable advantages, and generally treated Africans as children. This prejudice was part and parcel of the paternalist justification for colonial rule.[10]

The independence and bloody partition of India in 1947 was a sign that the era of European colonialism was coming to an end, and inaugurated a global movement to end colonial rule. European powers found that their colonies were not very profitable, and colonial residents found ways to demand a greater voice in colonial administration.[11] In Africa, a nominally independent kingdom in Egypt was overthrown by a group of military officers in 1952, and the new government under Gamal Abdel Nasser carved out a secular socialist compromise with a heavily Muslim population. Sudan negotiated its independence from Britain in 1956 and quickly fell into a pattern of military takeovers, echoed elsewhere as young officers saw themselves as modernizers, often with the encouragement of Cold War powers seeking allies. They learned that the Cold War tension between the United States and the Soviet Union had created a rift in global politics that gave newly decolonized countries a role to play in the balance of power.

In coastal West Africa, a growing class of Africans with a European education began to push for independence with a logic the European overlords found difficult to ignore. The educated class argued they were fully "civilized" according to European norms and capable of running their own government. Workers on large European-owned farms, loading docks, and railways learned how to use labor actions like strikes and slowdowns to push for better pay and conditions. Rural farmers and urban dwellers sought access to the advantages held by European plantation holders and foreign minorities.

The ideology of pan-Africanism linked these struggles, emphasizing that the borders between African countries were recent and the presence of Africans in the Americas was the result of the slave trade. These circumstances supported an ideology that crossed ethnic, geographic, and religious boundaries. Pan-Africanism

Figure 1.2 President Julius Nyerere of Tanzania with President Kwame Nkrumah of Ghana during the Organisation of African Unity (OAU) heads of government meeting held in Accra in 1965. © Tanzania Information Services/MAELEZO.

argued that the interests of all people of African descent were best served by uniting their efforts and erasing the divisions that racist European institutions had imposed. The poet-philosopher Léopold Senghor in Senegal, the scholarly journalist Nnamdi Azikiwe in Nigeria, the firebrand mobilizer Sékou Touré in Guinea, and the charismatic politician Kwame Nkrumah all espoused pan-Africanism and the end of colonial control.

Nkrumah became the model and in many ways the prophet of independence for sub-Saharan Africa. He created a nationalist movement in the British colony of the Gold Coast and pushed for negotiations that led to its independence under a British-style parliamentary government, with him as its prime minister. Nkrumah renamed the country Ghana after a medieval kingdom and sought to industrialize it through a socialist economic policy, but his rule became increasingly dictatorial as he marginalized both rival politicians and traditional authorities.[12] He was overthrown in a military coup in 1966 that he claimed was engineered by the United States' Central Intelligence Agency.[13]

In East Africa, aspects of Ghana's independence trajectory took different forms in each territory. Kenya faced the most violent episode, when a grassroots movement that became known as Mau Mau launched a militant campaign on behalf of landless peasants.[14] British colonial authorities declared a state of emergency and imprisoned thousands in brutal reeducation camps. More conventional anticolonial activists, Jomo Kenyatta most prominent among them, were jailed for suspected ties to Mau Mau. Eventually the British looked to Kenyatta and his colleagues to negotiate a peaceful path to Kenyan independence. Kenyatta became president after independence, managing a political system based heavily on ethnic patronage until his death in 1978.[15]

Political activism in Uganda was more muted because there were very few European settlers, and because leaders of the Buganda kingdom at the heart of the territory saw themselves as partners in governance with the British. But a northerner, Milton Obote, emerged out of a convoluted competition between political parties to become prime minister at independence. Obote set an ideological course inspired by Nyerere's socialism. However, his effort to suppress Buganda's royal house led to dictatorial methods that eventually brought his overthrow at the hands of an unpredictable sergeant named Idi Amin in 1971.[16]

Long before he went into politics, Nyerere had approached the anticolonial struggle in Africa in regional terms. And, since his student days, he had favored socialism as the best means toward broad-based economic development. This orientation emerged from ascendant intellectual trends in Africa during the mid-twentieth century: pan-Africanism and socialism encapsulated a wide variety of visions for developing influential and technologically sophisticated societies. The wave of independence in Africa seemed to offer the opportunity to pursue these ideals, even though few envisioned building an independent state on the basis of anything other than the colonial territory and government. Somehow they had to build a national identity, and it was hardly a blank slate. Colonial boundaries, interwoven ethnic and religious traditions, and undemocratic political institutions represented conflicting historical contexts that independence could not simply erase.

Coming of Age in an African Colony, 1922–53

The green hills overlooking the eastern shore of Lake Victoria are covered in massive granite boulders. Climbing to the top of one, you can see the shimmering blue of the lake through the misty air. Looking the other way, the dry plains of the Serengeti vanish into the distance.

People have lived on the shores of this lake since time immemorial. Two thousand years ago they cleared entire forests to make charcoal for smelting iron into steel hoes and spears.[1] Certain families held the honor of guarding sacred forests atop the highest hills. A well-regarded man could act as a leader. He consulted with the local elders and made decisions about what to do if the rains were late, the cattle were dying, or villages came under attack. For hundreds of years, young teenagers were initiated in the wild hills beyond the village to face their fears, learn the rules of adult life, and prepare for parenthood. When their household chores were done, young people socialized at village dances. Once every twenty years or so a new generation of elder men would walk the territory occupied by their people, mapping it out, laying claim to it, and assuring its fertility.[2]

The people of these hills came to be known as the Zanaki, a small group whose politics were built around a council of elders, prominent family men with a knack for oral argument.[3] They had nothing like the royal house of Buganda on the other side of the great lake, with its king and council of representatives. In the 1800s Maasai cattle herders invaded, stealing Zanaki cattle and grazing their herds on Zanaki farms. While their parents were cowed by Maasai military might, Zanaki youth admired the Maasai warriors and tried to copy their styles and their age-graded fraternities. Fashionable young men wore their hair in long elaborate braids, and young women collected colorful beaded jewelry.[4] Zanaki elders cooperated with Maasai demands, but proudly held to their own traditions of ensuring the fertility of the land.[5]

German missionaries, and soon German armies, arrived in East Africa in the late 1800s. They bought off some chiefs, conquered others, and assigned coastal Muslim agents to administer where there were no chiefs. They established a handful of colonies in Africa, the largest of them being a land known as Tanganyika, bounded by the Indian Ocean in the east and the Great Lakes in the west, Mount Kilimanjaro in the north, and the Ruvuma River to the south. German rule could be harsh, but it was spread thin, and they paid little heed to Zanaki lands. In the south the Hehe people under their king Mkwawa were battle hardened from decades of war with Ngoni and other southern people. They fought a guerrilla war with the Germans for five years.

Ten years later, the whole southern part of the territory broke into a violent uprising against German rule known as the Maji Maji Rebellion. Its leader claimed to have a medicine (*maji maji*, meaning "magical water") supposed to render the German bullets harmless. The medicine may not have had much effect on German bullets, but it did organize a diverse rebellion across the south, where German labor demands had disrupted the local agrarian economy. Another ten years later, in a distant battlefield of the Great War in Europe, African troops under German and British officers fought battles across the territory.[6] Very little of this touched Zanaki people, whose biggest security worry was still cattle rustling.

In 1922, Tanganyika was taken from Germany, together with its other colonies, and given over to the League of Nations as a mandate territory. The League handed Tanganyika to the British, who already governed in neighboring Kenya and Uganda. This horse trading was all done with European maps, and only a few literate people in Tanganyika knew much about why one set of European rulers had been replaced with another speaking a different language. Zanaki country was a backwater just beyond the newly opened diamond mines on the southern side of the lake. The British focused their attention on the fertile slopes of Kilimanjaro, where coffee grew well; the southern highlands, where tea and lumber seemed like promising products; and the hot plains stretching in from the coast, where top-quality sisal could provide ropes for British ships. These industries were desperate for workers. Young men from landless families traveled to these areas for work, hoping to bring home enough cash for a respectable marriage, or at least help their families pay the colonial "hut tax" that was designed to push them into wage labor.

The British set themselves to the task of governing the territory, and they looked for people who could serve in a more official manner as "chiefs" administering colonial policy. In Zanaki land the closest thing to a chief had been a respected rainmaker, which really meant a charismatic religious leader. The British preferred more innocuous men and found a few congenial elders to serve as chiefs, among them Nyerere Burito. British officials described him as "a gentleman of the old school . . . who dearly loves to chat about old times."[7] They put him on the colonial payroll and depended on him to ensure that people in his area remained co-operative, just as they did with similar "chiefs" across the territory.

The British called this setup Indirect Rule, and spent no little time congratulating themselves for how well they knew their subjects. It was an effective, if exploitative, mode of government. Its deeper impact was to use ethnicity as the basic organizational principle of governance. The policy in effect established "tribes" as political units, and left a divisive legacy that created conflict in many countries. The British felt themselves to be more civilized than everyone else and granted themselves all the privileges of overlords. But, at least officially, they did not see Africans as innately inferior. They believed their African subjects could benefit from education, especially the sons of chiefs, who could be expected to provide loyal leadership if they got a little British education under their belts. They educated the sons of chiefs for free.

An African Child

Chief Nyerere Burito had numerous wives, as was typical for men who had a bit of status in a culture that valued family, farming, and fertility. Burito sent more than one of his sons to school, but it was not immediately apparent that the second son of his fifth wife would be worth educating. The boy was born on April 13, 1922, in the midst of the long rainy season. Mugaya Nyang'ombe, his mother, named the baby Kambarage after a mythical ancestor who brought rain. The name was an auspicious one for a chief's son, as rain was a sign that he should take on his father's role. For the British, however, such local beliefs were less important than that he become a pliant administrator of the colonial order. Pliancy was the one trait they would not find in young Kambarage Nyerere.

Kambarage grew up on his father's hilltop homestead at the heart of the chiefdom known as Butiama. Running a homestead was a shared labor, under the nominal direction of a patriarch. Adults produced food and gradually incorporated children into productive tasks. Girls worked with their mothers, who grew and prepared almost all the food the home needed. Boys were generally given a few head of cattle to care for, and groups of boys from various families would wander up into the hills to pasture their little herds. Thus engaged, they could spend much time scrambling among the rocks, playing and roughhousing. Kambarage had a close friend in his age-mate, Bugozi Msuguri, who later took a Christian name, David. With bows and arrows, they hunted *pimbi* (rock hyrax), rabbit-sized rodents that lived under the rocks.[8]

All the cultures on the eastern side of Lake Victoria initiated children into age-sets of one form or another. When a group of children reached the age of initiation, their parents sponsored their participation in a camp where they were taught how to function in adult society, how to face fear, and how to deal with the opposite sex. Boys were generally circumcised. Although Msuguri was a little younger, he was placed in the same age-set as Kambarage. That year, initiates also faced another test of courage, apparently for the sake of "fashion." An elder expert filed their front teeth into points—a painful passage, and one that gave Kambarage's ready smile a distinctively upcountry character. At that age they could then accompany older siblings when they heard the sound of a drum announcing a dance in a neighboring village. Sometimes a generous family would donate a cow to be slaughtered for the occasion, and the young people could stay up the whole night, dancing, flirting, and feasting.[9]

Zanaki people have a reputation for being argumentative, probably as a result of their political system, which privileged the most convincing speakers among the elders. Long before he went to school, Kambarage had already learned to think and to speak. He was also a sharp player of the game *orusoro* (known elsewhere as *bao* or mancala), a popular pastime in the village. To play the game, you pick up stones from one of the holes on your side and drop them one by one into the following holes, all the way around to your opponent's side, where eventually you can collect them back. Requiring the forethought of chess, the game taught a lesson more appropriate to the politics of extended families than to the combative politics of opposing parties: in order to gain favors, you have to distribute them.

Between cattle herding, village debate, and orusoro, Kambarage learned lessons in responsibility, critical thinking, and strategy. A neighboring chief, Mohamed Makongoro Matutu, told Chief Burito that it would be worth sending Kambarage to school, at least as a companion for another of Burito's sons, Wambura Wanzagi, who already knew Swahili. Sons of chiefs were given spots at the newly built Mwisenge Primary School in the nearby town of Musoma, two days' walk from Butiama. In early 1934, a school vehicle carried Wambura and Kambarage to Musoma to learn how to read and write.[10]

A Colonial Education

Mwisenge Primary School offered Standards one through four. It was a basic education in reading, writing, and arithmetic in Swahili, which was a foreign language for young Kambarage. The books drew him in, and teachers remember him reading in quiet corners at all hours. Nyerere also began to accompany his friend Mang'ombe (later Oswald) Marwa to religious instruction in Roman Catholic Christianity, reluctantly at first and then with increasing interest. "There wasn't enough to learn," Nyerere remembered about those years of voracious interest in his expanding world. In only three years, he was the highest-achieving student in the Lake Region on the territorial exams.

A headstrong young teacher named James Irenge saw Kambarage's potential. Irenge invited Kambarage and a few other students to his cramped teacher's quarters in the evenings for a "special subject of politics, of history, of things of the past and how they were, and how we would be able to govern for ourselves." The teacher told the children parables of how a sparrow chased off the crows preying on her chicks, of the owl who scared off the other birds by just opening its eyes. "I was telling them we should remove the foreigners. . . . Guns by themselves, and cannon, we can't use. We are not experts with them. . . . We'll use another way, of just the lips. 'We don't want them!' All of us, 'We don't want them!' They'll leave."[11]

His political consciousness thus awakened, Nyerere found his way to the elite school in the territory, the Tabora Boys School, where European teachers expected their students to meet the highest standards of British education and disciplined them to respect the colonial social order. Colonial Tanganyika mobilized the labor of Africans for the sake of a tiny European population, and allowed a small class of Indians and Arabs to act as merchants. Within this structure they needed a small class of literate Africans as both clerks and chiefs to help administer the sprawling territory. This new class of aspiring chiefs at the Tabora School were taught to be prefects, whose authority was not to be questioned by their charges in the dormitories. Nyerere recalled trying to defend a fellow student from physical mistreatment at the hands of a prefect. The headmaster punished both by calling on Nyerere to cane the mistreated boy under the gloating eye of the prefect. Nyerere was eventually appointed a prefect himself.

Nyerere started a debating club, with some of his classmates, as an outlet for his truculent mind. They debated things like the tradition of bride-price, which was the transferring of cattle from the groom's family to the bride's as a means of sealing the marriage. Nyerere knew something about this, as his father had already arranged a marriage for him with a slightly older girl in Butiama named Magori Watiha, giving fourteen cattle lest he should die without providing a wife for this promising young son.

Informally, he and his schoolmates also debated other issues of interest to these sons of chiefs, such as whether patterns of decentralized chiefships across linguistic regions could be turned into something like small centralized kingdoms, a development that their British education taught was a step toward a higher civilization. He explored religion through his friends. Andrew Tibandebage was Catholic; Emanuel Kibira was Lutheran; Ali Abedi was Muslim. Chief Nyerere Burito died in 1942, and, after finishing at Tabora the next year, Kambarage went to Nyegina Mission near Musoma to be baptized into the Catholic Church. He took the name Julius, and for a brief time he considered becoming a Catholic priest.[12]

Upon graduating from Tabora, Nyerere was offered a place at Makerere College in Uganda to train as a science teacher. This was the only institution of higher learning in East Africa, and there he was surrounded by inquisitive children from chiefly families and mission schools throughout the region. He and Andrew Tibandebage led a Catholic student group and went on to organize the Tanganyika African Welfare Association as a secular gathering point for political debate. Eventually they made it a branch of the Tanganyika African Association (TAA), a lobbying group for civil servants and businessmen that had branches throughout the territory.

Nyerere took a great interest in the philosophy of John Stuart Mill, not least because Mill's thought provided a point of entry into the logic of British rule and a means to question it. By this time, Mahatma Gandhi's civil disobedience campaign was having a notable effect in Britain's most prominent colony by appealing to modern humanist values while mobilizing Indian masses with the guise of the common man. Nyerere also discovered Karl Marx and within a year of arriving in Uganda wrote a letter to the *Tanganyika Standard* endorsing socialism as the basis for the East African economy, insisting that African people were "naturally socialistic." All his debating practice had taught him the art of argument, and he twice won regional Swahili essay competitions. In 1944 his essay drew on Mill's philosophy to argue for a more equal place for women in African society and slyly used this logic to build a case for Africans to exercise a more equal status in colonial society.[13]

Catholic priests at the newly established St. Mary's Secondary School in Tabora bragged that Nyerere chose to work at the Catholic school rather than at his alma mater across town. He later said that he chose St. Mary's because of an insulting letter from the government warning him that he would lose salary and pension benefits if he chose St. Mary's. Throughout his life, such threats infuriated Nyerere, and his adult personality appeared in his adamant refusal of the government's offer: "If I ever hesitated, your letter settled the matter."[14]

The deeper reason was the pull of Father Richard Walsh, the headmaster at St. Mary's, who became a mentor to him. Walsh was a progressive-minded member of the Missionaries of Africa (known as the "White Fathers") who believed that "every man's work has an economical value equivalent at least to what he needs to live decently."[15] His views conformed closely to Nyerere's own egalitarian ideals. He encouraged Nyerere's political ambition and rallied support for him in the Catholic establishment, with the hope that a Catholic political leader would defend the Church under an independent government.

At St. Mary's, Nyerere and his college friend Tibandebage started a debate team and made a profound impression on a new generation of students, not only at St. Mary's but also among their debating opponents at Tabora Boys. Several members of Nyerere's future government first encountered him in Tabora. He also took his first journey to Dar es Salaam in 1946, to attend a TAA conference called to oppose a proposal by the British Colonial Office to create a legislative assembly for the whole of East Africa. TAA leaders feared a regional assembly would be dominated by Kenyan settlers.

Back in Tabora, the government assigned Nyerere, who was then the secretary of the local TAA branch, to report violators of postwar price controls. "When I reported a violation," he recalled, "nothing happened. So I lost interest." Anxious to challenge colonial prejudices, he also set up a cooperative store in town to compete with the Indian merchants who ran nearly all the shops. The short-lived store never really got off the ground, evidence of how the social habits and networks cultivated in the colonial racial hierarchy lent themselves to stubbornly different roles in the economy.

On his visits home, he still stopped in to talk politics with James Irenge, his primary school teacher from Mwisenge. With Irenge's encouragement, Nyerere met with Zanaki chiefs to advocate for the creation of a "paramount" chief, as other ethnic groups were attempting to do in colonial Tanganyika. The idea gained some traction, and many thought Nyerere would be well qualified for the office. Around the same time, Richard Walsh had successfully lobbied for a government scholarship for Nyerere to study science at Edinburgh University in Scotland. The application was delayed a year because the scholarship board did not accept Nyerere's claim that Swahili should count as his second language. During the intervening year, Nyerere was torn between a patriotic urge to serve his people at home and the desire for the unknown horizons of a foreign education. Irenge told him to go abroad, "so that when he would return, without doubt he would lead all of Musoma and not just Zanaki country."[16] With some hesitation, Nyerere finally took the advice of both his mentors to go to Scotland.

Around this time he was also introduced to Maria Waningu, a young teacher at Nyegina Primary School. She was the daughter of Gabriel Magige, a leading Catholic convert in a village not far from Butiama. Although reluctant to engage in bridewealth customs, Nyerere was able to recover the cattle paid to Magori Watiha's family and use them to cement an engagement with Maria. When he went to Scotland, Maria continued to study and teach, partially at the urging of Father Walsh, who thought she would be better matched to her fiancé if she knew a bit of English.

Exotic Scotland

Upon arriving in the United Kingdom in April 1949, Nyerere began lobbying to change his course of study from biology to political science, telling the program's administrators about a former teacher who advised that for him to study science "was like doing sculpture with a pen."[17] These could be the words of Father Walsh, who had arranged the scholarship, but they sound a lot like his cantankerous teacher at Mwisenge, James Irenge. He also lobbied to increase the stipend for his fiancée and family back home, who were facing rising food prices. The issue turned into a two-year bureaucratic fight, with Nyerere suggesting they could just provide him a loan to send money to his family. The issue finally found partial resolution a few months before his departure. His concern for his family may have betrayed a sense of guilt for leaving them behind, because he enjoyed the rest of his time there immensely, despite the cold Scottish winds in Edinburgh.[18]

He studied British history and philosophy, economics and political theory, and a history of the Chinese peasantry. Reading widely in classical, radical, and rationalist political philosophy, he found means to confront John Stuart Mill's thinking, which had helped justify British colonialism in the twentieth century by advocating liberty for "mature" people, but "despotism . . . in dealing with barbarians." Even so, Mill's observation of history's "cruel" lesson that the "earthly happiness of any class of persons, was measured by what they had the power of enforcing" was one that stuck with Nyerere throughout his career. He was also drawn to Thomas Hill Green's political philosophy, which aimed at a consensual resolution of Mill's contradictions based on the reciprocal obligations between citizen and state.

The entire experience in Edinburgh, intellectual, social, and political, offered a means to reflect on Africa's future at a distance, removed from its everyday challenges under colonial rule. "As a result of my choice of subjects I found I had ample time to read many other things outside my degree course, and I did. I also spent a great deal of time arguing with fellow students about everything under the sun except Marxism (which is above!). I did a great deal of thinking about politics in Africa."[19]

Many were impressed with his good-natured intelligence, and he took on a far more global view of politics than had been the case in his upcountry home. Scotland was an exotic place for a young African, filled with new landscapes and social customs. His political activity eased his longing for home, while new friends like Sidney Collins, his Jamaican tutor in moral philosophy, helped him find a new identity in a world as wide as the British Empire.[20]

He got involved in the Fabian Society, a group of democratic socialists inspired by T. H. Green's philosophy. At Fabian meetings and church lectures, he advocated for an end to racial discrimination in the colonies. The Europeans had only created "inter-racial chaos," he wrote in an essay for a Fabian publication. "I appeal to my fellow Africans to take the initiative in this building up of a harmonious society." Some years later a devoted member of the Fabian Society, Joan Wicken, traveled to East Africa to study the independence movements. She traveled with party organizers and decided to contribute to their cause.[21] After finishing her degree, she returned to become a political assistant to Nyerere. For the next thirty years, Wicken led an austere life in Dar es Salaam as Nyerere's loyal aide, critic, and speechwriter.

Taking Stock Back Home

Nyerere completed his master's degree at Edinburgh in 1952 and fixed his mind on getting involved in politics when he got home. When he arrived in Dar es Salaam in October, Maria was there to meet him, and they made their way back to Butiama. His first task, as much a practical one as a means of settling back into the soil of his homeland, was to build a house for Maria. It was a time to reconnect with his childhood friend Oswald Marwa while slapping mud mortar between the wood-fired bricks. "I had to take off my Edinburgh suit . . . and with my bare feet mix the sand and cement." Nyerere claimed this was Maria's way of making sure he hadn't changed too much in Scotland. They were married on January 21, 1953, at the Mwisenge Roman Catholic Church in Musoma.

They traveled back to Dar es Salaam, where Nyerere had a job at St. Francis High School in Pugu, near where the airport now stands. Pointing to his master's degree, he insisted on a yearly salary of 9,450 shillings rather than 6,300 shillings (equivalent to $8,200 versus $5,400 per year in today's dollars). This was still less than a similarly educated expatriate British teacher would make.

Within a few months he again got involved in the TAA, to get acquainted with the accelerating political developments in the territory. As opposed to prominent educated chiefs like Thomas Marealle and David Makwaia, Nyerere was willing to work with the reticent civil servants and businessmen of the TAA who had much to lose by their political activity. Unlike the chiefs, Nyerere set his sights on the whole diverse territory, not just the ethnic boundaries within which the British preferred to contain local politics.

Things began to move very quickly after that. In 1954 Nyerere and the young leaders of the TAA drew up a new charter for the Tanganyika African National Union (TANU), in preparation for the visit of a delegation from the United Nations Trusteeship Council. The UN delegation made a positive report, recommending independence by 1980 at the latest. TANU members received word of the report during the wedding of George Patrick Kunambi in January 1955, cutting the celebrations short as the overjoyed guests prepared to press their case for independence.[22]

In March, Nyerere was invited to New York to speak to the Trusteeship Council. Leading TANU members like Dossa Aziz and Paul Rupia contributed to his travel expenses, and Father Walsh helped clear the way for a visa. Nyerere told the Trusteeship Council that TANU's objective was to prepare people for independence, a task that required them "to break up this tribal consciousness among the people and to build up a national consciousness."[23]

Upon returning he was told he no longer had a job at St. Francis High School, as the colonial government had informed the Catholic leadership that they would not countenance a salaried teacher openly involved in oppositional politics. Nyerere then moved his young family back to Musoma, to the house of Oswald Marwa, and there he found time for a welcome rest. Father Art Willie, a new Catholic priest in town, hired Nyerere to teach him the Zanaki language for seven hundred shillings a month. Every day Nyerere walked into town to work with Father Willie on language and translation. He translated catechisms, hymns, and pieces of the New Testament into the Zanaki language.

Meanwhile, TANU activity in Dar es Salaam was bubbling up, with new organizers like Oscar Kambona, who sold TANU cards like a seasoned salesman, and

Bibi Titi Mohamed, who had a large group of women from the African quarters singing the praises of TANU. Bibi Titi became a minister of parliament after independence but was later accused of treason in a plot linked to Kambona, who became Nyerere's opponent in the late 1960s. Kambona had risen quickly to prominence in TANU and later served in several ministerial positions before falling out with Nyerere and going into exile.

In mid-1955, though, he traveled all the way to Musoma to urge Nyerere back to the fight. "When I got to Musoma," Kambona later recalled, "I found him sitting on the floor reading a book about Gandhi."[24] (Throughout his career Nyerere continued to take yearly vacations in his home village during the rainy season, removing himself from Dar es Salaam politics while he took stock of himself and his country.) In this intensely diverse territory, how could they bring independence without stoking the fires of racial hatred, ethnic division, and religious prejudice?

3

TANU and Tanzanian Independence, 1954–64

"Since my return to Tanganyika," Julius Nyerere wrote in 1955 to George Shepperson, his former lecturer in Edinburgh, "a few things have happened both to me personally and to the Territory." Nyerere delighted in wry irony and found humor in downplaying the impact his political activities had already brought in Tanganyika. He had finished at Edinburgh in 1952 and returned home soon after. Now he had catapulted to prominence and was known across the territory as a standard-bearer of the burgeoning independence movement.

But in this letter he wrote more about his marriage with Maria and the birth of his first two children. He blandly mentioned his election the previous year as president of the Tanganyika African Association (TAA), "a sort of socio-political organisation," he explained. "In July last year we transformed this into the Tanganyika African National Union [TANU], a fully fledged political organisation which pledged itself to work for self-government."[1]

TANU's birth on July 7, 1954, is now regarded as a momentous occasion, and the date is still celebrated as

Tanzania's preeminent national holiday, known as Saba Saba (or "Seven Seven") Day. It seemed less impressive at the time. That sunny Wednesday morning in the dusty town of Tabora just happened to be the day that an African lobbying group changed its name. But within ten years TANU would control an independent African country, arm liberation movements in Southern Africa, and fend off Cold War intrigue in Zanzibar by annexing that island territory to create a new nation, called Tanzania.

Nyerere went on to explain in the letter that, "as a result of the visit to New York, I lost my job and am now [a] jobless gentleman organising TANU." His modesty here served a purpose. He knew that TANU's birth and its future fortunes were not his alone to claim. The growth of TANU was the work of a large group of dedicated men and women who saw themselves not as colonial subjects, but as citizens of a future nation. Muslims and Christians from various parts of the territory, their ethnic and religious differences were of little concern. They set their sights on gaining an African voice in territorial politics. Without these colleagues, Nyerere might well have become an influential educator in Tanganyika, maybe even a politician, but not its transformative first president.

The Birth of TANU

In the early 1950s a group of "Young Turks" took over the leadership of the TAA, a twenty-year-old organization representing the interests of a tiny African middle class of educated civil servants and businessmen. They were anxious to communicate their concerns about the colonial government's proposals for political reform, which seemed designed to keep African influence to a minimum for decades to come. The new TAA leadership consisted of recent Makerere graduates like Vedastus Kyaruzi, who had been involved in student politics, and older World War II veterans who were now Dar es Salaam businessmen and civil servants like the Sykes brothers, Ally and Abdulwahid.[2] Compared to their elders, both groups were much more sophisticated in dealing with European thought and culture, and much less intimidated by the colonial state.

Channeling the activism of its upcountry branches, the new leadership submitted a memorandum to the government protesting any attempt to develop the Tanganyika political system in a way that would give different rights to different racial groups. They proposed a process that would lead to a freely elected government in control of internal affairs by 1962. Through patient negotiation and energetic politics, they got their wish, despite the colonial government's best efforts to slow their ambitions for self-government.

Nyerere was well known to the TAA's young leaders because he had studied with some of them. They arranged for his election as president of the TAA in April 1953. They thought he could help reverse the decline of the TAA, which had fallen on hard times, victim to subtle government intimidation and the rising radicalism of other organizations. The Meru Citizens' Union peacefully brought its case for land reform all the way to the United Nations, while some World War II veterans spoke of "going to the forest" to start a guerrilla movement.[3] Nyerere was concerned that rising militancy in some upcountry districts would lead to clashes with the colonial government. He believed that Tanganyika could be liberated from colonial rule, but that violence would only delay independence and sabotage the freedom that followed. He wanted to avoid forcing the government into a defensive crouch, as had happened in Kenya because of the Mau Mau rebellion there.

Nyerere worked with Kyaruzi and the Sykes brothers to rewrite the TAA constitution for its transformation into TANU. They made it a more effective umbrella organization that could coordinate the efforts of various African political groups and better control the policies and statements of branch offices. The new constitution declared their intention to "build up a united nationalism" and "fight relentlessly until Tanganyika is self-governing and independent."[4]

"The Atmosphere Has Been Suddenly Revolutionised"

At the July 1954 conference, Nyerere pointed out that since Tanganyika was technically a UN trust territory and not a British colony, they owed no allegiance to the Queen of England. So, when a UN delegation came back with a positive report and recommended independence within the next twenty-five years, the TANU leadership took it as an endorsement of their ambition for independence. They deftly brought about a peaceful transition in a fraction of that time.

Nyerere toured the country, giving speeches and meeting with branch leaders, and was soon recognized across the territory as the face and voice of TANU. At the grassroots level, TANU's energetic women's and youth wings made the party into a political juggernaut across the territory. TANU activists Bibi Titi Mohamed and Oscar Kambona led an organizing drive that built up TANU's membership from two thousand members at the beginning of 1955 to over forty thousand by the end of the year. By 1960, it had over a million dues-paying members. The party's leaders vowed, "Even the smallest child in the village should know the meaning of TANU and freedom."[5]

Women and youth joined the movement enthusiastically compared to adult men, who feared for their jobs.[6] Traveling across the country, young activists established a nationalist vision in songs and friendships that crossed ethnic and religious boundaries. Young people served as the "guards for all occasions," translating the widespread culture of youth serving in military roles into a modern political equivalent.[7] Women, especially urban Muslim wives and mothers, were organizers, caterers, and hosts for campaign events small and large, goading their husbands into active support for the movement.[8] Nyerere sought advice from women like Bibi Titi Mohamed, the

Figure 3.1 Chief Minister Julius Nyerere with Bibi Titi Mohamed (*center foreground*), Umoja wa Wanawake (UWT) chairperson Sophia Kawawa (*right*), and Maria Nyerere (*far right*).
© Tanzania Information Services/MAELEZO.

most prominent of the Dar es Salaam mobilizers; but also the politically active British-American widow, Lady Marion Chesham, who hosted his entourage when he came to Iringa; Barbro Johansson, a Swedish educator in the Lake Province; and a witty young mother from Kilimanjaro, Lucy Lameck, who went on to serve in numerous positions in the party and in government after independence. All of them served in the independence parliament.

The blustery British governor of Tanganyika during this time, Edward Twining, appealed to traditional chiefs to counter TANU's popularity. The chiefs depended on government support for their authority and income. Such "traditional authorities" were the foundation stone of British colonial policy. The effect of this policy was to entrench ethnic divisions by granting chiefs their small "tribal" spheres of influence and diverting political activity into ethnic associations. TANU leaders asked people to ignore ethnic divisions and unite for the sake of democracy and independence. Twining labeled this "extreme nationalism" and "nothing more than racialism," hypocritically ignoring the racial order that allowed a few friendly chiefs to represent millions of Africans in a European-dominated Legislative Council. The chiefs who opposed TANU only added to people's distrust of all colonially appointed authorities. This served Nyerere's goal of building up a unified national sentiment across the territory, and he constantly repeated TANU's slogan, *Umoja ni Nguvu* (Unity is Strength). TANU flags decorated houses in cities and villages across the country.

Twining regarded Nyerere as an adolescent upstart, and Nyerere outwitted him at every turn. The governor's ham-fisted hostility toward TANU played into Nyerere's hands. "[Twining] opposed us, thus giving us a foil," Nyerere recalled, "yet he only once barred me for three months from speaking all around the country!" If TANU's struggle with Twining was a chess game, both sides still had their best pieces on the board in 1958, when Nyerere unexpectedly maneuvered Twining into an unwinnable position.

The governor had arranged for what he thought would be a predictable election that would pack the Legislative Council with friends of the government while appeasing the African majority with token representation. His "tripartite" scheme was to allow every educated person to vote, including Africans, but each voter had to vote for three representatives for the council: a European, an Asian (Arab or Indian), and an African. This provided a façade of democratic participation, but it also assured that the council would still be dominated by Europeans and Asians, who were presumed to support the government's gradualism. This structure, Twining hoped, would defuse TANU's pressure for full democracy.

TANU members saw through Twining's tripartite ruse, and many wanted to boycott this election of a "half-caste government." Nyerere realized that a boycott would only marginalize TANU and legitimize the government's division of people into racial categories. After an initial hesitation, he fought for TANU's participation. At a TANU conference that year he swayed the assembly with the type of folksy political speech that allowed him to charm audiences throughout his career. Nyerere compared the tripartite election to a big mud puddle between a farmer and his field. "If you want to harvest your crops and carry them out of the field you must first step into the mud and dirty your feet."[9] His humor swayed undecided members, whose laughter drowned out the remaining advocates of the boycott.[10]

One of those who still supported the boycott was Zuberi Mtemvu, a long-standing TANU member who left the party in protest and went on to start his own party called the African National Congress. Mtemvu's ANC advocated "Africa for Africans" and became TANU's main opponent as independence approached. Various political parties, reconstituted chiefdoms, and labor unions struggled for influence in the late colonial period. TANU's broad popularity allowed it to sideline most competitors, but their alternative visions often took root amidst jostling factions within TANU.

TANU cleverly recruited European and Asian supporters in the 1958 elections and campaigned on their behalf. With TANU's massive influence, the elections turned out a new council packed with members of every race, all backing TANU's nationalist policies. Much to Twining's chagrin, he woke up to find a legislature controlled by TANU and pushing for independence. A TANU newsletter proclaimed the victory with an apt Swahili aphorism, mocking Twining's tripartite trick: "If a child cries for a knife, let him cut himself." Nyerere wrote a letter to supporters in Britain, telling them that the "atmosphere has been suddenly revolutionised. . . . They know that TANU is invincible as long as there is no violence in the country."[11]

For Twining this was the end of the road. He was replaced by a new governor, Richard Turnbull, who had witnessed the horrifying clash of insurgent violence and government repression in Kenya. Turnbull was ready to work with Nyerere for a peaceful transition in Tanganyika. Despite disagreements with the new governor, Nyerere estimated that "we both want an atmosphere in

Tanganyika in which political controversy, however hot, can take place in peace and dignity." A new British government in London under Harold Macmillan was also keen to unload its colonies in Africa, which were relics of an earlier era and a burden to the Treasury. Macmillan caused great offense in the all-white South African parliament when he told them bluntly, "the wind of change is blowing through this continent, and whether we like it or not, this growth of national consciousness is a political fact."[12]

Faster than they had planned, the British bent to TANU's pressure and promised "responsible government" after elections in 1960. This meant that elections would be fully democratic, and the new legislature with its chief minister would have full authority over Tanganyika's internal affairs. TANU won again handily and Nyerere became the council's chief minister. In an expeditious constitutional conference, legislation for an independent government was drawn up over the course of one day, on March 27, 1961. On December 9, 1961, with much pomp and ceremony, Tanganyika became an independent member of the British Commonwealth, in full control of its internal and external affairs, with Nyerere as its first prime minister. They planned another election for one year later, when the country would break its administrative ties with the British Crown and declare itself a republic. His generation had been born under European rule, and for the first time in their lives they had the chance to shape their own destiny.

Figure 3.2 The Constitutional Conference, March 1961. *From left (facing camera):* Minister of Agriculture Derek Bryceson, Minister of Education Oscar Kambona, Legal Advisor Roland Brown, Chief Minister Julius Nyerere (*standing*). © National Archives, UK.

The Animal Called Independence

Amidst the euphoria of independence, the sobering task of governing weighed heavily on Nyerere. Since 1958, the TANU leadership had grown more familiar with the inner workings of the colonial government. Despite its repressiveness and foreign imposition, life in the place known as Tanganyika was bound to this government, and no nostalgic fantasy could bring about a return to a precolonial past. In any case, there were few who imagined or even wanted to go back in time. Most looked toward the future, but independence brought a

52

particularly fertile ground for new imaginings. A new society was there to be formed, with many competing visions of what it should look like and how it should function. It was a time of "too many pied pipers," recalled the labor organizer Peter Kisumo.[13]

Speaking to an audience shortly before independence, Nyerere's words were lighthearted but his message was serious. He compared TANU's drive to independence to a successful hunt:

> When hunting there is no problem, other than
> maybe someone gets wounded by an arrow, but
> that is not a big problem. Problems start when the
> animal has died, that's when fighting starts, because
> this one wants that piece and another cuts another
> piece, and that's when people start to get their fingers
> cut. This is the difficulty of having a Prime Minister
> in the country; the hunters, in this case, are you,
> the labor unions, TANU, cooperatives etc. We have
> cried for independence without difficulty. Now that
> this animal called Independence has fallen, conflicts
> begin.[14]

It was a particularly colorful illustration, for his agrarian audience, of concerns he expressed in more academic terms at the United Nations. A key task for TANU was "to build up national consciousness" that could transcend ethnic and religious identities. In Nyerere's mind, this meant the suppression of divisive politics. He contended that legitimate opposition aimed at improving government functions, but that it always remained "loyal" to the country. He insisted that a "supreme authority" elected by a popular majority had the right to control a "dissenting minority" if necessary. Shortly after independence Nyerere told journalists that if any group based their opposition on race, religion, or tribe he would "lock it up—and if I did not have a law to do so, I would make one."[15] He promptly endorsed a Preventive Detention Act that allowed the government to imprison people indefinitely without charging them with a specific crime.

TANU had campaigned on a platform of democracy, but Nyerere was prepared to suppress opposition politicians if campaign events became so heated as to threaten the country's peace or its economy. He feared that if prompt progress were not made to improve people's lives, or if the government failed to integrate its uneducated rural population into national political institutions, a small spark of disagreement could be fanned into a violent conflagration. That fear justified his authoritarian urges, which only grew as he consolidated power. As the break with Britain approached, Nyerere advocated a one-party state for the first fifteen years of independence.[16] This suggestion invited protest from opposition figures like Zuberi Mtemvu who feared for the fate of democracy under TANU's dominant majority. Mtemvu's protests against his marginalization were justified, as Nyerere's government repeatedly blocked his political campaigns.

Independence was a moment of great hope and a time of quiet fear. Tanganyikans, especially its politicians, looked anxiously at what had happened in the Congo. There, independence came abruptly in 1960, and its most popular politician, Patrice Lumumba, was brutally assassinated within months. The Congo exploded into violence fueled equally by the Cold War and by separatist political ambitions in regions that had been only loosely bound by a colonial state. Vedastus Kyaruzi, a physician and a colleague since their time in the TAA, recalled visiting Nyerere one day and finding him "extremely tense" as he contemplated the Congolese situation. Nyerere abruptly asked him, before he could go, "Doctor, shall we succeed?" Kyaruzi reassured Nyerere that he had broad support across the country, unlike Congo's violent regional competition. His encouragement reflected a common solution to the problem of political division in postcolonial Africa, the personalized focus on a single leader, often to the detriment of a democratic opposition. Gathering up his courage in the face of Lumumba's cruel fate, Nyerere sang a verse from a coastal bridal song: "Don't cry, baby, you yourself chose, you yourself decided."[17]

On another occasion, Kyaruzi inquired about Nyerere's thoughts on the increasingly ambitious demands of the labor movement. Nyerere responded, with an authoritarian bite, "The duty of government is to govern. We are going to govern." From 1960 to 1962, Nyerere suppressed both Mtemvu's Africanist opposition and a labor movement that threatened to derail Tanganyika's nascent economic growth. These years brought a rash of labor walkouts that peaked in 1960 when hundreds of strikes added up to 1.5 million lost days of work.[18] Nyerere worked closely with Rashidi Kawawa, a leading figure of the Tanganyika Federation of Labor (TFL), to moderate labor's demands.

More ambitious labor leaders continued to resist government attempts to temper their demands and allied themselves with Zuberi Mtemvu's ANC party.[19] The ANC was pushing for a more aggressive policy of replacing British civil servants with Africans, a process known as Africanization. TANU's moderate leadership suspected the calls for rapid Africanization were a thinly veiled form of racial discrimination.[20] But many in TANU's rank-and-file gazed upon European civil servants and settlers with veiled resentment and questioned their right to be citizens of the new African nation. Nyerere countered racial resentment by making sure that his cabinet included people from various religions and ethnic groups, including white and Indian representatives.

When legislation was presented in the Assembly that would limit citizenship only to people of African descent, Nyerere was indignant and threatened to resign if the law passed. He argued that once racial bias was introduced to Tanganyikan politics, its logic would take on a life of its own: Congo's wars were driven by ethnic claims to autonomy, Hitler's Germany had committed genocide in the name of ethnic purity, and similar rhetoric had already taken root in Rwanda. The apartheid police state run by a white minority in South Africa under Hendrik Verwoerd had created the conditions for catastrophe. Visibly angry, Nyerere laid out his points in the starkest possible terms.

> A day will come when we will say all people were created equal except the Masai, except the Wagogo, except the Waha, except the polygamists, except the Muslims, etc. . . . You know what happens when people begin to get drunk with power and glorify their race, the Hitlers, that is what they do. You know where they lead the human race, the Verwoerds of South Africa, that is what they do. . . . Sir, what is the crime in the world today? It is the oppression of man, by man. It is the treatment by those in power, of those who have no power, as if they are goats and not human beings. . . . That is what we have been fighting against. . . . I have said, Sir, because of the situation we have inherited in this country, where economic classes are also identical with race, that we live on dynamite, that it might explode any day, unless we do something about it. But positively, not negatively. . . . I am going to repeat, and repeat very firmly, that this Government has rejected, and rejected completely any ideas that citizenship with the duties and rights of citizenship of this country, are going to be based on anything except loyalty to this country.[21]

Nyerere threatened to resign and thereby derailed the race-based citizenship law, but the issue smoldered just below the surface. At a TANU conference six weeks after independence, Nyerere repeated his resignation threat in protest against those in TANU still pushing for race-based policies. This time, he followed through: to nearly everyone's surprise, the charismatic politician who had led the country to independence abruptly quit his office. But his closest colleagues knew he had another goal as well. Lest TANU's powerful grassroots organization be forgotten in the rush to control the government, he wanted to rebuild the party into a populist anchor for his vision of national unity.

Nyerere handed over the post of prime minister to Rashidi Kawawa, who decisively took the reins of government on Nyerere's behalf. He oversaw the passage of restrictive labor legislation, the Preventive Detention Act, and the drafting of a republican constitution.[22] Smart, self-effacing, and tough, Kawawa continued as Nyerere's most trusted associate for fifteen years. In the meantime, Nyerere traveled the country, visiting TANU branches and talking with people, and this may have been his intention the whole time. He wanted to ward off racialist sentiment, build up nationalist loyalties, and define an ideology to guide TANU as a governing party rather than a protest movement.

During this year of upcountry travel, Nyerere read a book by Petro Itosi Marealle an old man from a chiefly family near Mount Kilimanjaro. The book presented a theory of rural African society that the author called *ujamaa*, meaning "familyhood." Nyerere first

Figure 3.3 Second Vice President Rashidi Kawawa, in his office, mid-1960s. Courtesy of the Borthwick Institute for Archives, York, UK.

used this term in a speech on land policy a few months after his resignation. He began to develop Ujamaa into a comprehensive political ideology that combined African nationalism with his own unorthodox theory of harmonious socialism that rejected Marx's theory of class conflict. Nyerere envisioned African socialism as a social ethic derived from the shared responsibilities of family life in rural Africa. It relied on a hopelessly romantic vision of precolonial society, and was very much a political invention, but it was effective. This new rhetorical strategy made it possible for anyone of any race or religion to lay claim to authentic membership in an African nation, simply by showing themselves to be "people of Ujamaa." Ujamaa became Nyerere's governing ideology for his entire period in office, taking on a life of its own as the much-debated orthodoxy of Tanzanian politics.[23]

Another strategy to bridge the contradiction between African cultural authenticity and the suppression of ethnic division was the promotion of Swahili as a national language. To encourage people to learn Swahili, Nyerere had long insisted that TANU campaigns be conducted entirely in Swahili, without someone translating speeches into local languages. The government now moved to make Swahili an official language next to English. Although some members of parliament continued to address the assembly in English, gradually its business came to be entirely conducted in Swahili, as well as nearly all functions of government except high court cases.

Because of their linguistic diversity, most African countries depended on a colonial language—primarily French, English, or Portuguese—as the only language all its citizens shared. Tanzania had the advantage of Swahili as a widely understood trading language. With its heavy load of Arabic vocabulary and a common root with the widespread Bantu languages, it was relatively easy to learn for most people. Like Ujamaa, the official use of Swahili gave people the sense that the independent government was theirs, and not just a continuation of colonial imposition. In order to demonstrate its suitability for government business, Nyerere translated Shakespeare's *Julius Caesar,* and later *The Merchant of Venice,* into Swahili.

In the November 1962 elections, Nyerere won 98 percent of the vote—which was not surprising, given the harassment of the opposition—to become president of the Republic of Tanganyika. This meant that the colonial governor was withdrawn and the government had no more formal ties to the Queen of England beyond those of normal diplomacy. Nyerere optimistically took it to be a rejection of Mtemvu's race-based politics and an endorsement of Ujamaa.[24] But, in suppressing the opposition, Nyerere also stifled necessary public debate about policy and ideology.

Nyerere wore his emotions on his sleeve. His joy, anger, and sadness often poured out into public view. After seeing off Governor Turnbull at the airport in December, Nyerere gathered with friends and family at his home. The American ambassador William Leonhart stopped by to deliver a message of congratulations from the American president. Nyerere read the message aloud in Swahili and then took the ambassador's hands and led him aside, telling him, "I was all right until I said my last good-bye to Turnbull this morning. It was what I wanted, but I almost broke down. For the first time, I felt alone."[25]

Independence in the midst of the Cold War was an intimidating prospect, but Nyerere had established himself and his party firmly in power. He now turned his attentions to Tanganyika's external relationships. Diplomacy in the US and Europe yielded significant foreign aid. Closer to home, Nyerere maintained that

Tanganyika's independence would not be complete until the entire region was free of colonial control and domination by racist minority regimes. Dar es Salaam hosted the Liberation Committee of the Organisation of African Unity (OAU)—which managed funds, supply chains, and armament delivery for movements across the region, while sorting out their internal disputes. Nelson Mandela came to visit, and the government tried to mediate disputes among Rhodesian nationalists and give them radio broadcasts and weapons to aid their struggle.[26] Nyerere personally recruited Eduardo Mondlane to head up the Frente de Libertação de Moçambique (FRELIMO), a new militant movement to liberate Tanganyika's southern neighbor, Mozambique.[27]

Nyerere also wrote two letters to American president John F. Kennedy. The first explained that South Africa's racist policies were a threat to peace across the whole of Africa. The second argued that regional federation was the best response to the pan-Africanist sentiment that sought to transcend the limitation of colonial territories by uniting African peoples. Federation would create larger units that would have more influence on the world stage.[28] Impressed with Nyerere's eloquence, Kennedy invited him for an ostentatious state visit. The two young Catholic presidents hit it off well, but the visit produced little of substance. Kennedy was not prepared to do anything significant to change South Africa's policies, since the apartheid regime was a strategic US ally in the Cold War. Nyerere's visit to Washington did little to ease his weariness with "pomposity," which he complained was already getting out of hand in Tanganyikan officialdom.[29] In London he chose to do without the "swarms of motor cyclists buzzing around distinguished visitors as they do in the United States."

After meeting members of the British government and greeting representatives of the royal family, Nyerere took the opportunity to enjoy a rare night of anonymity. He and his British press secretary decided to go on a "pub crawl" in London's East End, where they met a gregarious pub owner who took them for a walk, regaling them with tall tales of the neighborhood's history. "They managed to put back a good deal of beer and had got on famously," Nyerere's secretary reported. "The interesting thing was that the pub manager had no idea who the President actually was!"[30] It was also the highlight of the London visit, which, like his visit to Washington, produced little of substance. For all of Nyerere's eloquence, Tanganyika remained a small fish in the big frozen pond called the Cold War.

1964: The Fragility of Freedom

By the end of 1963, the Tanganyikan government had fallen into a comfortable rhythm and was effectively addressing the multitude of challenges it faced as best as it could with the limited resources available. Following up on World Bank recommendations to transform the rural sector, rural "villagisation" experiments got underway by gathering farmers to build "modern" villages.[31]

The government introduced legislation to establish a National Youth Service program that would channel the energies of Tanganyika's youth—especially the rambunctious members of the TANU Youth League—into paramilitary training and public works. Africanization had begun in earnest, and the policy was making steady progress in replacing outgoing British expatriates in civil service positions.[32] Nyerere had become frustrated with the reluctance of his colleagues in Kenya and Uganda to move forward on an East African federation, but still hoped for greater regional cooperation. Within the country, however, it seemed as if Tanganyika's bloodless transition into independence could not have gone more smoothly.

At least until 1964: The new year brought the sort of trials that condemned many new African countries to endless conflict. Creatively responding to one crisis after another, Nyerere stabilized his government and kept the country at peace.

Nyerere had always been uncomfortable with the racial rhetoric surrounding Africanization policy and now pushed for "localisation" of the civil service, meaning that the effort would be to hire and promote citizens of Tanganyika, regardless of their race, to replace the highly paid expatriates. On January 7, 1964, Nyerere announced that "discrimination in civil service employment, both as regards recruitment, training, and promotion, must be brought to an end immediately."[33] The one branch of government where Africanization had not made a significant impact was the army. The entire officer corps was still British and its British commander was in no hurry to promote African officers. Rank-and-file soldiers heard Nyerere's announcement and wondered if the army had been left out of Africanization. Taking a page from the labor movement's combative playbook, a few noncommissioned officers began to think about ways to make their voices heard.

Meanwhile, in the predawn hours of January 12, a ragtag group of proletarian revolutionaries raided a police station in Zanzibar. The radical youth league of the Afro-Shirazi Party (ASP) had been planning a revolution for over a year. They joined forces with a delusional Ugandan immigrant named John Okello who had recruited a small army of frustrated plantation workers.[34] Crowning Okello as the "Field Marshall," they seized weapons, took over strategic locations, and embarked on a short-lived reign of terror.

The tensions leading to the Zanzibari Revolution had been brewing for years. In January 1964, various groups of populists, nationalists, and communists converged to spark a transformative change of government that upended political relations up and down the East African coast. The islands of Pemba and Unguja lie just off the Tanganyika coast, and from 1890 until December 1963 they constituted the British colony of Zanzibar. Revolutionary fervor boiled over when Britain granted independence to a government under a figurehead prime minister whose parliamentary coalition of landed interests was portrayed by populist politicians as nothing more than a return to the slave regime of the former Arab sultan. But for many, even among the peasants, the sultan remained the symbol of Zanzibari sovereignty.[35]

During the last decade of colonial rule, bitter and sometimes violent electoral politics had raged around resentments between those who felt at least partially bound to their indigenous African roots and those who identified most strongly with their Arab heritage. The lines between these deeply rooted groups were in constant flux, but had solidified amidst the vengeful politics of the early 1960s.[36]

The leader of the ASP, Abeid Karume, was a former sailor and bandleader with a knack for populist performance. He had the broadest base of political support. Karume slipped away from the islands the morning of the revolution and returned a few days later to take control of Okello's formless government and put an end to the massacres that had left thousands of Arab Zanzibaris dead or in exile. Karume reached out to Nyerere, who sent a large police contingent to stabilize the new government and ease the unpredictable Okello into exile.

A week after the revolution, while Nyerere lounged at a State House reception for the new Zanzibari leaders, his own army mutinied. Inspired by the dramatic events in Zanzibar, the mutineers imprisoned their British officers, took control of the airport and telegraph office, and marched up to the State House in search of the president. Nyerere got word of the mutiny just before the soldiers arrived and was spirited away to a Catholic mission across the Dar es Salaam harbor. With much of the police force in Zanzibar, the government could do little but negotiate with the mutineers. Nyerere's ministers conceded to their demands for better pay and accepted their African nominees for commanding officers. Within two days, Nyerere returned to the State House and toured the city, exuding a sense of normalcy. He scolded the mutineers for undermining Tanganyika's stability and told the press that his first priority was to "win back the reputation we had as a peaceful and mature country."[37]

When copycat mutinies took hold in Kenya and Uganda, British-led troops quickly suppressed the disorder.[38] British diplomats offered the same support to Nyerere, but he was reluctant to ask the former colonial power for help, as if his newly independent country could not take care of itself. The turning point came when evidence emerged that radical labor leaders were urging mutineers to go beyond their demands for Africanization and higher pay and instigate a coup d'état.[39] Nyerere then turned decisively to British help. The British prepared an efficient commando strike overnight and attacked the mutineers' barracks the following morning. Within hours they had disarmed the mutineers, who were helpfully hungover from a celebration organized for them the night before. Nyerere then detained hundreds of labor activists for questioning. Some were released within weeks, others languished in prison or home arrest for years.

For Nyerere, the mutiny and its resolution were not only a great shame but also a sign that his government's stability could not be taken for granted. He was not so much concerned about being pushed out of power, but that a rebellion would undermine everything that he had worked for and everything Tanganyika had become. Many compared the mutiny to Congo's problems and shuddered to think that harmonious Tanganyika could so easily have started down the road of lawlessness. The violence in Zanzibar only heightened these anxieties. The "African Cuba" off the Tanganyikan coast had caught the attention of the Cold War superpowers, whose interventions in the Congo had so quickly overwhelmed that country's nascent political institutions. The task ahead, as Nyerere and his colleagues saw it, was to ensure governmental stability in Tanganyika and Zanzibar and prevent superpower interests from taking control of political events in East Africa.

The following months brought intense interest in Zanzibar from the US, the Soviet Union, and China. East German military advisers moved in quickly after the revolution, while British and American spies recommended military intervention. Nyerere and his colleagues worried that the US might try to replace the revolutionary Zanzibari government with a puppet regime of the former sultan's loyalists.[40] They were equally worried that the Soviet Union or China would use military aid to turn the new Zanzibari government into a launching pad for communist revolutions on the continent.

Nyerere had long tried and failed to bring any of the new East African nations into a federation. In Zanzibar he saw a chance to use the dream of federation to achieve a more immediate purpose. Several members of the new Zanzibari government had come to Dar es Salaam in January to talk with foreign minister Oscar Kambona about a union between the islands and mainland Tanganyika. By April, superpower pressures were such that Nyerere and Karume agreed to a hastily prepared union treaty, which they signed on April 22 with no public consultation or referendum. On April 23, they abruptly announced that they had created the United Republic of Tanganyika and Zanzibar. The union offered Karume a stronger counterweight to East German influence and caused the US and Britain to back away from plans for military intervention.[41]

Within days the treaty was unanimously ratified by the Tanganyikan Legislative Assembly and pushed through the Zanzibari Revolutionary Council. "Can't you see," explained one Tanganyikan minister, as the countries slowly negotiated the practical arrangements of united government, "what we have done is first to build a roof. . . . After that, the window, walls and doors will come."[42] Even though he was later critical of the way the union was structured, Karume's successor as Zanzibar's president, Aboud Jumbe, saw no alternative at the time to its hurried creation. "In 1964 the people were not consulted because the two leaders were in a race against time and could not afford the luxury of delay."[43] It was not until several months later that they even agreed on a name for the new entity: the United Republic of Tanzania.

The awkward union treaty was modeled on the relationship of Northern Ireland to Great Britain, and was destined to be troublesome. It created a union government of Tanzania and a separate semiautonomous government for Zanzibar, with no Tanganyikan counterpart. Zanzibar would retain Abeid Karume as its president, and he would also serve as the first vice president of Tanzania. Nyerere became president of the United Republic; and the Tanganyikan vice president, the ever-loyal Rashidi Kawawa, was given the title of second vice president. It was a makeshift solution that relied on Nyerere's international prestige to keep the superpowers at bay in Zanzibar, but it seeded a legacy of continued resentment among many Zanzibaris who blamed their postcolonial travails on what seemed like a crass attempt by Nyerere's government to annex the islands.

The creation of Tanzania was not a favor to any of the Cold War powers, but rather a move to keep their conflicts out of East Africa. Nyerere could tell the American ambassador that he had "arrested the rot" in Zanzibar by blocking communist infiltration, but socialist influence in Tanzania's government only grew.[44] Nyerere respected the intellect of Zanzibari radical Abdulrahman Babu and felt that "Babu had the ideas necessary for thoroughgoing social reform," even if he worried that Babu desired a more dogmatically communist revolution than Nyerere envisioned.

Within a year, Nyerere began building a strong relationship with communist China and provided military aid and training to movements struggling to overthrow white minority governments across southern Africa. At a press conference that year he poured out his frustrations about external interference: "The maximum risk is [that the] army will revolt. My army revolted in January. It was not trained by Chinese. . . . The Chinese want to colonize Tanganyika, my foot! It is humiliating that I have to explain to Ambassadors any decision about accepting seven Chinese instructors. I do not expect other people to take decisions for this government. I am completely capable of looking after this country."[45]

Clearly, the nation of Tanzania was a very personal project for Nyerere. In ten years, the "jobless gentleman organising TANU" had become a statesman of international stature. At the UN in 1955, he had told the Trusteeship Council that TANU's main objective was internal: "to build up a national consciousness among the African peoples in Tanganyika." Ujamaa was one means of cultivating nationalism, but the turmoil of 1964 reinforced Nyerere's fear that all could be lost in a moment if the government failed to protect its sovereignty. In the years to come, this line of thought led him down ever more authoritarian paths as the government hardened into the one-party system that he had proposed before independence. During the debate over the Preventive Detention Act, Nyerere insisted, "If we succeed in creating a nation, we can stand criticism. But if we fail we will be ridiculed."[46] His words betrayed his concern that excessive political competition could undermine national unity, but they also spoke to the deeply personal stake he had in a government and nation that he had nurtured from its inception.

Nyerere and his colleagues had built a peaceful nation and defended it against threats both internal and external, but its economy was still dependent on external aid. Without economic independence, political independence was a fragile thing.

4

Ujamaa and the Race for Self-Reliance, 1965–77

The events of 1964 shook Nyerere deeply. In the January mutiny, the republic he had worked so hard to build seemed ready to collapse in an instant. International intrigue at the end of the year had left him feeling suspicious even of people he considered as friends, like his colleague Oscar Kambona and the American ambassador William Leonhart. Internally and externally, his government became increasingly distrustful and security-conscious.

The fragile union with Zanzibar was a cunning response to Cold War pressures but did not put an end to them. By 1965 his part of the world looked like a far more dangerous place than it did in 1960. In response, Nyerere sought to strengthen the state. He accelerated the establishment of single-party government, inserted party personnel into the army and state-owned industries, and brought labor unions, youth movements, and religion denominations into close alliance with party policy. Even if Nyerere still welcomed criticism within the party, his consolidation of power meant he could impose his vision on society rather than negotiate with opponents. Decisions came quickly, but without the moderating effect of political process.

His most effective initiative may have been the elaboration of his political philosophy into policy. Ujamaa allowed him to strike an independent path through Cold War ideological battles between capitalism and communism. It was the ideological equivalent of his nonaligned foreign policy, and its notion of familyhood demanded that Tanzania come to the aid of its neighbors rebelling against minority governments. Nyerere pursued a regional strategy from the beginning, believing Tanzania's independence to be thoroughly tied to that of its neighbors. Ujamaa provided an ideological anchor and a "national ethic" for a government that people could consider their own and not just the remnant of a little-loved colonial state. Nyerere argued that with Ujamaa there would be no need for opposition parties dividing people and wasting valuable political energy.[1] Single-party elections in 1965 seemed to deliver on the promise of this vision when a number of senior officials were ousted by local upstarts. That such upheaval became the norm indicates that some degree of real choice held sway in Tanzania's single-party elections.[2]

Ujamaa became the reference point for all political debate. It provided a rationale for taking control of foreign businesses. It justified surveillance of political leaders in the name of eliminating corruption and inequality. It drove an attempt to bring scattered villagers into larger settlements under more direct government control. Most importantly, it became a way to manage political factions that otherwise tended to pull him too far in every direction. The Tanzanian state became an Ujamaa state. The ideology brought unity and discipline to the young government, but also excess.

Ujamaa: A Political Invention

Nyerere had taken an interest in socialism since his days at Makerere University in the 1940s. Back home in Butiama, he had long conversations with Father Richard Walsh, the Catholic priest who had helped arrange for his scholarship to study at Edinburgh, about how to preserve the virtues of traditional life in a changing African society. Both of these lines of thought shaped his approach to independence: the new nation needed a "national ethic" that would guide people's thinking about governmental policy and the rights and responsibilities of citizenship in the new nation. Nyerere took Petro Itosi Marealle's term "ujamaa" and expanded it to include his social philosophies combining aspects of rural African custom, utilitarian philosophy, and socialism. Ujamaa came to mean Nyerere's own idiosyncratic theory of "African Socialism."[3]

Defining his own theory of socialism allowed Nyerere to free himself and his society from the bipolar extremes of the Cold War as well as the constraints of Marxist orthodoxy. Rooting his theory in a nostalgic vision of village life, Nyerere could define socialism as a unifying force for independent Africa rather than a divisive one. It also provided him a powerful claim on socialist credentials without the need to follow Soviet or Chinese precedents. Ujamaa gave him a philosophical independence to match the new nation's political independence.

> European socialism was born of the Agrarian
> Revolution and the Industrial Revolution which
> followed it. The former created the "landed" and
> "landless" classes in society; the latter produced the
> modern capitalist and industrial proletariat. These
> two revolutions planted the seeds of conflict within
> society, and not only was European socialism born
> of that conflict, but its apostles sanctified the conflict
> itself into a philosophy. . . . African socialism . . . did
> not start from the existence of conflicting "classes"
> in society. . . . The foundation, and the objective,
> of African socialism is the extended family. . . .
> "Ujamaa," then, or "familyhood," describes our
> socialism. It is opposed to capitalism, which seeks
> to build a happy society on the basis of exploitation
> of man by man; and it is equally opposed to
> doctrinaire socialism which seeks to build its
> happy society on a philosophy of inevitable conflict
> between man and man. . . . Our recognition of the
> family to which we all belong must be extended
> yet further—beyond the tribe, the community,
> the nation, or even the continent—to embrace the
> whole society of mankind. This is the only logical
> conclusion for true socialism.[4]

It was a powerful rhetorical strategy. Ujamaa became the language of politics in Tanzania and the appeal to idealized family values captured people's attention throughout the country. Initially it was a means of focusing diverse ideas about how to build a modern nation out of a colonial state in a multicultural swath of East Africa. Ujamaa pulled political debates toward the categories Nyerere defined, but eventually began to drag Nyerere's ideological moderation into its own increasingly radical current.

In the last years of colonial rule, a World Bank study had recommended the "transformation" of the rural sector, and various theories of development promoted the creation of more concentrated village settlements where the state could implement social services like education, health care, and agricultural support.[5] Nyerere and his colleagues articulated this vision through Ujamaa, putting forth a utopian vision of rural peasants living and working together, sharing village-owned farming equipment and working communal farms with scientific methods. In a society where most of the people were rural farmers, this seemed like the best way to make the most of their skills and experience while building up a robust economic base. It was a way for Nyerere to focus governmental policy on rural society and make sure that the division between educated urbanites and illiterate peasants did not threaten the unified nation TANU had built.

Another way to infuse Ujamaa into the society was the National Youth Service, known as the JKT—the

Jeshi la Kujenga Taifa, or the Army to Build the Nation. Several Tanzanian ministers had seen national youth service programs in countries like Ghana and Israel, and now adapted the idea to Tanzania.[6] They saw the program as a modern analogue of the widespread custom of *jando*, of sending youth off into a wilderness camp for a time as part of their transition to adulthood. Instead of learning local customs, youth learned Ujamaa.

The JKT was voluntary at first, but, beginning in 1965, secondary school graduates were required to spend two years in the JKT. This entailed a period of quasi-military training, followed by work on rural roads or farms, and then a public service job at minimal salary. In 1966, students at the University of Dar es Salaam marched to the State House in protest against reduced salaries during their two-year national service requirement. Nyerere met the marchers and berated them for their sense of privilege, asking how many of them ate so well at home. Citing Shakespeare's *The Merchant of Venice,* Nyerere continued:

> But you want your pound of flesh. . . . The meaning
> of National Service is that the nation is asking the
> youth for its services. The youth does not turn to
> the nation and say "how much" and then sit down
> and bargain. . . . It is not forced labor for a teacher
> to be in a classroom earning £380 a year. . . . You are
> right when you talk about salaries. Our salaries are
> too high. . . . I'll slash the damned salaries in this

country. Mine, I slash by twenty per cent, as from this hour. . . . These are the salaries which build this kind of attitude in the educated people! Me and you! We belong to a class of exploiters. . . . I have accepted what you said. And I am going to revise salaries permanently. And as for you, I am asking you to go home.[7]

With that he sent the students back to their upcountry homes, where they stayed for over a year until they were reinstated. The confrontation with the students revealed Nyerere's frustration with the growth of a new class of African elites, the "'nizers," who were seen as beneficiaries of the Africanization effort to replace foreign civil servants and managers with local employees.[8]

The Arusha Declaration

Nyerere's emotional confrontation with the students stemmed from more than just their resistance to national service. Several of his colleagues also observed the rise of a class of civil servants who sought and expected personal gain commensurate with their status. Party leaders began working on a policy that they hoped would restrain wealthy elites, limit corruption, and accelerate economic growth. In Ujamaa, Nyerere had created his own idiosyncratic theory of African socialism, but it was more a quasi-religious statement of his desire for a "national ethic" than an actual policy.

Since the Zanzibari Revolution, Tanzania had lost the support of several of its Western donors and began moving steadily toward socialism. When West Germany cut off military aid in protest of Tanzania's plan to host an East German consulate in Dar es Salaam, an enraged Nyerere told the West German ambassador to "take the rest of your aid as well."[9] In 1965, Nyerere broke relations with Britain to protest its passive policy toward Southern Rhodesia's declaration of independence, which had made it easier for the white minority there to maintain its domination. The break made him seem vulnerable to Portuguese observers, whose spies suggested that he was unstable and feared a coup d'état.[10]

In order to free Zambia from economic dependence on Southern Rhodesia and South Africa, Nyerere had been lobbying for help to build a railroad from Dar es Salaam to Lusaka.[11] The US and Britain were willing to build roads, but refused to sponsor a railroad.[12] Nyerere also visited China for the first time in 1965 and brought home an agreement for the Chinese to build the Tanzania-Zambia railroad. Chinese teams moved in within a year and began planning a thousand-mile route through the difficult terrain of southern Tanzania. The Chinese gave assiduous attention to the project. Construction began in 1970 and was completed ahead of schedule in 1975 for $400 million, accounted as an interest-free loan to Tanzania.[13]

Impressed by the austere attitude of the Chinese bureaucracy, Nyerere began to envision a socialist state modeled on the one built by Chairman Mao. Consulting with a few trusted party members in late 1966, Nyerere began work on a policy statement committing Tanzania to a more radical socialist path.[14] He proposed nationalized industries and communal farming, while at the same time constraining the economic activities of political leaders as a means to fight corruption. Binding these two themes together was strategic. The nationalization of industry appealed to socialist radicals, who presented an increasingly influential critique of global capitalism combined with a vision for rapid modernization. State-owned industry was also attractive to those who looked at government service as an economic opportunity. The lure of managing a parastatal business helped ease the passage of what came to be known as the Leadership Code, a series of rules that made it nearly impossible for civil servants and paid party officials to maintain any private business for personal gain.

On February 5, 1967, at a party meeting in Arusha, Nyerere announced this policy in a dramatic speech that came to be known as the Arusha Declaration. "We have been oppressed a great deal, we have been exploited a great deal," he told the party members. "It is our weakness that has led to our being oppressed, exploited, and disregarded." Declaring "war against poverty and oppression," and socialism as a "belief" and a "way of life," Nyerere called for a "revolution to end our weakness." He offered a resounding ideological defense of a socialist strategy. The speech also contained a cogent critique of Tanzanian society and warned prophetically of the threat that an urban elite in control of policy could become an exploitative class. His reasoning reinforced his concern for rural society. Tanzania remained pre-eminently a society of peasants whose interests were at risk of being ignored.

> Our emphasis on money and industries has made
> us concentrate on urban development. . . . To repay
> the loans we have to use foreign currency which
> is obtained from the sale of our exports. But we
> do not now sell our industrial products in foreign
> markets. . . . It is therefore obvious that the foreign
> currency we shall use to pay back the loans used in
> the development of the urban areas will not come
> from the towns or the industries. Where, then, shall
> we get it from? We shall get it from the villages and
> from agriculture. What does this mean? It means that
> the people who benefit directly from development
> which is brought about by borrowed money are not
> the ones who will repay the loans. . . . If we are not
> careful we might get to the position where the real
> exploitation in Tanzania is that of the town dwellers
> exploiting the peasants.[15]

The Arusha Declaration was a turning point in Tanzanian history and a widely influential speech in Africa. The speech defined the terms of political debate in Tanzania, and was initially widely popular in the country. But there were also voices of dissent. The most prominent political figure to come out against the Arusha Declaration was Oscar Kambona. Although initially supportive of the policy, Kambona was almost alone when he openly opposed the socialist vision, even though many quietly agreed with him.

Kambona's fate became a demonstration of the ideological power Nyerere had created with the Arusha Declaration. Kambona had resigned from the cabinet the previous year when Nyerere appointed him Minister of Local Government and Rural Development. He then left his position as secretary general of TANU, in apparent protest against the Arusha Declaration.[16] An element of demagoguery emerged in Nyerere's reaction to Kambona's resignation and the wider resistance toward the Arusha Declaration. Responding in kind to vituperative attacks from Kambona's allies, Nyerere called them "madmen," "prostitutes," and "mercenaries." Just days later, fearing arrest, Kambona fled the country into exile in London. The details of Kambona's defection remain unclear. The Tanzanian government justified his denunciation with a confidential claim that he had left the country with $700,000 in unreported funds, while public disclosures put it in the range of $100,000.[17] In any case, Kambona came out as a fierce critic, accusing Nyerere of dictatorship in bold speeches in Europe and Africa.[18] Kambona became the focal point for a number of politicians who resisted Nyerere's radical turn and his increasing capacity for authoritarian action.

In absentia, Kambona was charged with treason, while Nyerere reiterated the condemnation of Kambona as a "thief" and a "prostitute." He was accused, with a group of sympathetic party members and military officers still in-country, of planning a coup. Kambona's exile and the treason trial provided a window into deeper tensions in the Tanzanian state. Other members of parliament were expelled during this time, ostensibly for common crimes and corruption, but many protested that they were being punished for mere dissent. For Nyerere, the lines between friendship, ideological allegiance, and political loyalty became blurred; these seemed like personal betrayals by men he considered friends. To them, it felt like Nyerere had sacrificed friendship and democratic debate for his own political ambition. Although Nyerere's ostensible goal was to eliminate corruption from the party and government, the effect of these aggressive tactics was to entrench authoritarian habits and squelch debate about the dangers of socialist policies.

Nyerere's ideological control in the one-party government allowed him to sideline opponents at will. When a mob killed nine cattle thieves in 1969, sixty-five people were arrested, of whom seventeen were found guilty. One of the accused was a popular politician and a friend of Nyerere's since high school, Joseph Kasella Bantu. Bantu had made an incendiary speech, but the judge found that the speech neither advocated nor sparked the killings, and he was acquitted. He nonetheless remained in detention for months and was detained repeatedly over the next decade. Like many civil servants, Bantu was upset about the pay cuts Nyerere had instituted during his confrontation with the university students, but also the concentration of power in the small group of loyalists surrounding Nyerere in the party Central Committee. At the trial, and subsequently, Bantu accused Nyerere of using character assassination to destroy opponents and socialist policies to cripple politicians who disagreed with him.[19]

Nyerere's socialist trajectory, with the takeover of church schools and hospitals, cost him support among some of his Catholic supporters as well. For Nyerere personally, Ujamaa may have had a spiritual element, but his mentor, Father Richard Walsh, frowned on a trend of socialist atheism among students in the early 1970s. The nationalization of church schools was an extension of a policy put in place after independence to help shrink the gap between Christian and Muslim levels of education by opening schools to children of all religious faiths. Nationalization made all schools non-denominational, while allowing children to get religious instruction in their chosen faith.[20]

The Arusha Declaration set Tanzania on an economic path that eventually proved disastrous. Within days the government began to nationalize banks and major industries. The main weakness of the policy was that it fell upon a strained civil service with limited economic expertise to plan an entire economy. It faced the same problem of planned economies everywhere: politicized production priorities were a poor substitute for the market signals that businesses relied upon to

Figure 4.1 President Julius Nyerere with Premier Zhou Enlai of China, 1965. © Tanzania Information Services/MAELEZO.

gauge their growth. At the time, however, the powerful speech was a visionary call to economic "self-reliance" and social equality. Nyerere had solidified his place in Tanzanian politics as the "Mwalimu" whose words carried the same sort of weight as those of Chairman Mao in China. Although Nyerere pursued his own ideological path, China was clearly the model for national administration.

At the local level, Nyerere found his model in a southern village. During his trip to China, Nyerere brought along a member of the TANU Youth League, John Ntimbanjayo Millinga, from the isolated region of Songea. In response to Nyerere's call for people to set up agricultural settlements, Millinga led a group of young people to found a remarkable communal farming experiment in 1962. After a difficult start, they were eventually joined by a sympathetic British farmer who had been working in Southern Rhodesia. They set up a series of villages where farmers worked small individual plots and also participated in large cooperative farms. With Millinga's thoughtful leadership and some outside financial help, they gradually expanded their Ruvuma Development Association (RDA).[21]

RDA members shared not only equipment, resources, and training, but also decision making. Seeing the need to train their children to participate in the project, they set up schools oriented toward practical training. Nyerere got word of the project and visited in 1965. Impressed by their new constitution, which laid out the operation of the growing movement, he offered his approval and a little bit of material aid. He visited again in 1966 and encouraged his colleagues to do the same. He told the RDA leaders that TANU was going to come up with a policy that would promote more projects like theirs.

The Arusha Declaration was published early the next year, and in a series of pamphlets Nyerere laid out a policy for Ujamaa villages that followed closely on the model of the RDA, from their cooperative governance to their vocational goals for schooling. He even hired Millinga to head a new TANU department of *Ujamaa Vijijini* ("Ujamaa in the Villages"). Nyerere ordered TANU Central Committee members to pay extended visits to the villages and brought RDA members to other parts of the country to teach others about their approach. Politicians in Songea and Dar es Salaam resented Nyerere's insistence that they learn from what seemed like a group of uneducated young peasants.

In front of the party's Central Committee, Nyerere occasionally pointed to Millinga as the only real socialist among them. This annoyed the TANU leadership, and, despite Nyerere's strong support, they turned against the RDA. While they mouthed support for the model, party leaders argued that the independent movement had to be subsumed under governmental authority so that the model could be applied uniformly across the country. Nyerere mocked the petty reasons the Central Committee members gave for breaking up the RDA, but eventually capitulated for the sake of party unity, in the hope that it would allow the RDA model to be seeded throughout the country.

In September 1969, Central Committee members traveled to Songea and arrested the leadership of the RDA, ending its independent existence. The policy of Ujamaa Vijijini struggled forward, with the government offering incentives for villages to implement Millinga's model, but they had none of the self-reliant enthusiasm of the RDA. Millinga remained in office but struggled to find a place among the powerful bureaucracies of the party and government.

Using Nyerere's writings as their instrument, party officials and government bureaucrats herded peasants into new villages. Usually this meant that poor families had to build new houses and farm new fields using unproven methods. Occasionally, skilled community leaders could inspire a measure of devotion to Nyerere's vision, but villagization rarely improved production. It mostly served as a means for local officials to gain power over heretofore self-sufficient small farmers. Although some observers found that women gained a measure of security in the compact new settlements, in many cases it meant that a council of men made decisions for the village and women had even less of a voice than they had had in their rural homesteads.[22] The policy foundered without clear direction until Nyerere decided to jump-start it with even more force in 1973.

Villagization as an Order of the Party

A variety of issues pushed Nyerere to accelerate villagization in the early 1970s, but the dominant concern was how to reverse a long-term decline in the country's external balance of payments that began after the Arusha Declaration. For Nyerere, maintaining a healthy reserve of foreign exchange was a key measure of economic success. Without foreign exchange he was forced to rely on external grants and loans and could not pursue the "self-reliance" that he perceived as necessary for Tanzania's sovereignty.[23]

The policies of the Arusha Declaration were meant to increase agricultural exports while building up light industry to produce consumer goods that the country had been importing. But with its lack of foresight, the policy had the opposite effect. The country had to buy more imported machinery to build up an industrial base, and the new parastatal industries never produced enough to make a dent in Tanzania's balance of payments. The only immediate way to make a positive impact on foreign exchange reserves was to increase cash crop production, and the only positive areas of export production were in tea and tobacco.

Placing his faith in the World Bank transformation model, Nyerere chose villagization at all costs to mold a modern countryside. As he told the 1973 TANU conference, "Eleven years . . . eleven years since we started making all this noise about living together in villages. . . . [T]he issue of living in villages is now an issue for the whole country." This pronouncement was translated in the party newspaper to read, "The issue of living in Ujamaa villages is now an ORDER of the party." Those who were reluctant to move were labeled as opponents of the party, and villagization policy entered its final and most controversial phase. With the logic that "it is not easy to change the ideas of peasants," even Nyerere dismissed his own insistence that change must come only with the initiative of community members.

Without local ownership of community administration, as had been the case in the RDA, the policy proved a disaster. In some areas the transformation amounted to nothing more than registering an existing village as an Ujamaa village. In other areas regional administrators began telling rural residents to pack up within days.

Government lorries and Field Force police arrived to transport people at gunpoint and dump them unceremoniously on the empty sites of new villages.[24] Many villages were established along roads, ostensibly so that they could more easily transport their crops. Often such villages were just hastily erected façades that a regional commissioner could present when Nyerere came to visit. Ill-considered planning often put people far from their fields and sources of water, a particularly difficult issue for women who had to care for children, contribute to communal labor, and tend to their own subsistence farms.

Some thirteen million people, the vast majority of the rural population, were registered in seven thousand villages. According to a government survey in 1978, none of them achieved the official targets of Ujamaa policy. The policy so disrupted rural farm production that many villages depended on famine relief for years and there was wide evidence of increased malnutrition. Food imports skyrocketed, depleting the foreign exchange reserves that the policy had proposed to fill. Between the scramble to procure scarce foodstuffs and government expenditure on villagization, inflation accelerated, hitting 75 percent in 1974. It was not intended as a policy to starve the peasantry, and the government worked assiduously to distribute food and other social services to the villages, but even this had an element of coercion: to get the food and services, people were required to move into villages.[25]

In retrospect, it is still hard to understand why villagization was forced upon the population with such haste in the mid-1970s. Thoughtless village planning paid little attention to the impact of the program and its viability in marginal lands. Many families continued to keep livestock, and the compact settlements led to overgrazing and the disruption of traditional ecological management.[26] The scholar Goran Hyden suggested that traditional economies centered on the family farm, or *shamba*, tended to undermine nationally directed agricultural policies.[27] In retirement, Nyerere echoed this insight: "You can socialize what is not traditional. The *shamba* can't be socialized."[28] Some observers note that the generous aid from foreign countries allowed Nyerere to pursue disastrous policies that would have otherwise collapsed quietly in their inception.[29]

Many of Nyerere's colleagues still insist villagization was the only way to organize rural communities in order to bring them social services. In this respect, it had some moderate successes. The villages provided focal points for infrastructural improvements by aid organizations like OXFAM, and nodes of governance across the rural countryside.[30] Health-care facilities in rural areas expanded rapidly, sometimes exceeding targets. During the 1970s the government more than doubled the number of health centers to reach 239, and nearly doubled the number of rural dispensaries to reach 2,600. The number of rural health-care workers tripled to serve these facilities. This expansion still could not reach every village in a rapidly growing population, and the drive to quickly increase the quantity of health services came to the detriment of quality.[31]

The government also built schools in pursuit of an equally hasty policy of Universal Primary Education (UPE). When the government first began expanding education, it aimed to get all children into primary school by 1989, but then it abruptly accelerated the target to 1977. Because of villagization it was possible to claim that 80 percent of children were in schools by 1978. But this haste had the long-term effect of lowering the standards for primary education, leaving rural schools in woeful condition.[32] But there was no way to train more teachers other than by first expanding primary education, and in a basic sense UPE and adult education programs were an enormous success. No other African country could boast of near universal literacy as Tanzania could by 1980.

The 1970s brought Nyerere to the peak of his power both domestically and internationally, but it was also a decade of enormous frustration. He told an audience in Denmark that "Tanzania has tried to keep a balance between its urgent need to increase the amount of wealth, and its conviction that the purpose of wealth is man, who must not be destroyed in the process of creation."[33] Villagization had upset this balance and violated Nyerere's repeated statements in support of popular participation in decisions affecting people's lives.

Figure 4.2 President Julius Nyerere greets a member of the Ujamaa Group in the Junior TANU Youth League, ca. 1975.
© Tanzania Information Services/MAELEZO.

The Burdens of Leadership

An external measure of Ujamaa and its pan-Africanist ideals was Tanzania's commitment to aiding African rebel movements in the white-dominated states of Southern Africa. This effort stemmed from Nyerere's long-standing view that freedom in his own country was only guaranteed when the entire continent was free from minority rule.

Most visibly, the settler governments in South Africa, Southern Rhodesia, and the allied Portuguese colonies in Mozambique and Angola were insults to African pride in an era of decolonization. Tanzania's leadership in support of the liberation movements bolstered Nyerere's militant credentials and helped him outflank those who criticized his good relations with Western countries. The liberation struggle was key to Nyerere's ability to forge an independent foreign policy amidst the superpower rivalries of the Cold War. Beyond Southern Africa, however, he was a prominent voice against militarism, criticizing American action in Vietnam as well as the Israeli occupation of Palestine. In both cases he urged the withdrawal of forces and a negotiated settlement.[34]

Nyerere was more restrained in his criticism of the indigenous dictators and military governments that sprouted across the continent during this period. Although he bitterly denounced the separatist leader of the Congolese state of Katanga, Moise Tshombe, who hired mercenaries from South Africa and elsewhere, Nyerere tolerated his corrupt successor Joseph Mobutu, who controlled the Democratic Republic of the Congo (or Zaire, as he renamed the country in 1971) for thirty years with American backing. He remained a firm friend to Uganda's Milton Obote, whose Common

Man's Charter closely followed Tanzania's ideological path, despite Obote's attempts to consolidate dictatorial power.[35] When the brutal military leader Idi Amin pushed Obote from power in 1971, Nyerere refused all relations with his new nemesis. Nyerere accused Amin, who expelled the entire Asian (mostly Indian) population from his country, of being an African fascist, just as racist as the white South African government.

Yet anti-Asian sentiment continued to bubble in Tanzania as well. Nyerere spoke forcefully against Amin's action and against racial scapegoating at home.[36] But when a boatload of Asian refugees from Uganda approached Tanzanian shores, the government refused to take them in.[37] Nyerere struggled to balance his inclusive principles against populist voices. A letter published in the government-controlled national newspaper described Asians as questionable citizens who "need[ed] tough handling."[38] In order to contain anti-Asian sentiment, Nyerere agreed to a law nationalizing all buildings worth more than one hundred thousand shillings in order to eliminate "landlordism." On its face, it was not a racially directed policy, but in effect it was an attack on the Indian commercial community, who owned most of these buildings. Nearly fifteen thousand Asian citizens and residents left within months. In the first decade of Tanzanian independence, the African population of the country had doubled, while the Asian population had fallen by half, to less than sixty thousand. Those who remained felt bitter, betrayed by a leader they had trusted but who now seemed to be acting like an Idi Amin in disguise.[39]

Amin represented exactly what Nyerere had most feared for independent Africa, violent xenophobic rule by populist dictators with no education who appealed to people's worst instincts. He could tolerate more canny dictators, like his northern neighbor, Jomo Kenyatta, who spoke with moderation even as he shored up his support with ethnic alliances at home and loyalty to Western powers abroad. Tensions with Kenya were not about personality or even ideology, but largely concerned nuts-and-bolts negotiations over the East African Community, an economic union formed in 1967 that fell far short of the political union that Nyerere was trying to build. Given their different economic policies—Kenya's head start in industry, Uganda's descent into chaos, and Tanzania's intense financial troubles by the mid-1970s—the EAC faced too many obstructions to cooperation and collapsed in June 1977.[40]

The most complicated relationship Nyerere faced was right at home, where Abeid Karume's increasingly arbitrary rule and race-baiting rhetoric turned the semiautonomous region of Zanzibar into a petty police state of star chambers and public executions—where Karume's idea of racial harmony was apparently to be achieved by demanding that the daughters of local Arab and Persian families marry loyal politicians.[41] Karume had ably managed the transition from violent revolution to authoritarian governance, but seemed ill-prepared to

Figure 4.3 President of Zanzibar and First Vice President of Tanzania Sheikh Abeid Karume, ca. 1965. © Tanzania Information Services/MAELEZO.

do much else. He surrounded himself with thugs and yes-men and hounded the few thoughtful politicians who remained into watchful silence. When Zanzibari politician Othman Shariff fled to the mainland following Karume's denunciation, Nyerere gave him an upcountry veterinary job, while his more inflammatory colleague Kassim Hanga was imprisoned on the mainland.[42] They were both flown back to Zanzibar in 1969 under uncertain circumstances with a flimsy promise that they would receive a fair trial. Instead, they were mocked in a stadium show trial and executed within days.[43] Although Karume was an embarrassment and a threat to the humanist ideals of Ujamaa, Nyerere saw little choice but to tolerate the dictator for the sake of their shared government, which was increasingly fragile.[44]

In 1972 Karume was assassinated by a disgruntled military officer ostensibly angered by the detention of his father.[45] The assassin worked with a group that clearly represented a large swath of Zanzibari society who could not tolerate Karume's erratic rule any longer. Despite its potential for destabilizing violence, the assassination was certainly a relief to Nyerere as well, and he built a much more productive relationship with Karume's successor, Aboud Jumbe.

Few would deny that Nyerere also became a dictator during this period of tremendous upheaval on the African continent. He maintained his authority without mass violence, but the powerful Special Branch of the police force kept close tabs on dissent, and the paramilitary Field Force ensured that strikes, protests, and grassroots resistance didn't interfere with government policy. Many government officials, including regional commissioners, had the power of preventive detention even if all detentions were eventually reviewed by the president's office. Citizens and politicians were regularly detained for corruption: some for mere dissent, a few for actual subversion, and many more just because they had angered someone powerful in the local government. Nevertheless, cautious criticism of government policy found voice regularly in print, in parliament, and within the party.

A British man who spent three years in Tanzanian prisons in the 1970s said that his fellow prisoners estimated there were around five hundred political detainees among them during this period, plus a thousand military personnel imprisoned for discipline infractions. Other political prisoners were housed in secret detention centers. In order to manage the prison population, the government regularly granted mass amnesty to common criminals and would quietly release political prisoners among them. In 1981, after one such release, Amnesty International estimated that less than one hundred prisoners remained incarcerated under the Preventive Detention Act, down from its estimate of over one thousand detainees in 1977. While detention officers and even higher officials were occasionally prosecuted for abusing detainees, there is little doubt that torture was common in detention cells. Even so, it seems that Nyerere enforced a prohibition on extrajudicial killing of political prisoners, and most mainland detainees survived their captivity. Common criminals did not benefit from the same oversight. Conditions in the overcrowded prisons were atrocious, rife with abuse and sometimes death from maltreatment.[46]

In the end, Nyerere's power rested on a broader base, one that depended more heavily on ideology than intimidation. But even here, with all his rhetorical gifts, he barely kept the upper hand. After Amin's takeover in Uganda and the populist swell in Tanzania that accompanied the nationalization policy, TANU radicals passed a new set of guidelines that aimed to eliminate the last vestiges of capitalism. The *Mwongozo*, as the guidelines were called in Swahili, inserted party officials between workers and management. Industrial disputes turned bitterly personal. Managers found it easier to appease workers than insist on sound business practice, while cynicism about the policy resulted in corruption. As a result, good management became nearly impossible in the many publicly owned industries created or confiscated since the Arusha Declaration. The economy became increasingly chaotic, with chronic shortages and wasted investment.[47] In reaction to the breakdown of industrial discipline, the government only increased repressive policies in a fruitless effort to recover economic growth.

Political repression in Tanzania also grew from the intrigues of the militarized liberation movement and fears of subversion. Militancy kept the country on a continual war footing and justified the authoritarian tendencies of Nyerere's government, as paranoia infused local attitudes toward foreign visitors. By the mid-1970s, strategic advantage began to shift to the African "Frontline States" that supported the rebel movements. The collapse of Portugal's military government in 1974 and its withdrawal from its colonies represented a major victory in the liberation struggle for Southern Africa. A friendly socialist government under Samora Machel and FRELIMO took root in Mozambique, but it faced ongoing conflict with rebels supported by South Africa, based in southern Mozambique and Rhodesia. Likewise, Angola struggled with a protracted civil war between the MPLA government of Nyerere's ally, the left-wing nationalist Agostinho Neto, and American-supported rebels under Jonas Savimbi and Holden Roberto.

Negotiations over Southern Rhodesia creaked forward without resolution. American and British politicians knew no agreement would hold without Nyerere's approval, and he was adamant about what negotiators called NIBMAR (No Independence Before Majority Rule).[48] American secretary of state Henry Kissinger visited twice. He and Nyerere found in each other worthy adversaries, and despite their disagreements each expressed his admiration for the other's political acumen. Tanzania supported rebel military activity, pushing the US faster than it wanted to proceed in Africa. But Kissinger was a realist, and despite the American preference for a more gradual course, he knew the endgame was near. He later wrote admiringly of Nyerere's subtle tactic of endorsing militarism while holding out the possibility of a diplomatic "miracle."[49]

The election of Jimmy Carter brought new energy to the Rhodesian negotiations, as the new American president, deeply devoted to human rights, was willing to oppose South African interests in the region. In 1977, Nyerere made his second state visit to the United States, where Carter welcomed him with glowing praise, noting how his stature had grown since his first visit with John Kennedy: "He is admired in every country . . . a senior statesman whose integrity is unquestioned . . . a man who has forgone material wealth and ease in a sacrificial way for his own people." In Atlanta, just before his

Figure 4.4 President Julius Nyerere greets Coretta Scott King in Atlanta, 1977. © Tanzania Information Services/MAELEZO.

departure, Nyerere visited the grave of Martin Luther King Jr. with his widow Coretta Scott King. "I did feel it was important," Ms. King told a reporter, "that Julius Nyerere, who is a real liberation fighter, and Martin Luther King, who espoused nonviolent means to freedom, blend their spirits together."[50]

Despite the accolades, it was a period of great stress and overwhelming activity. Nyerere's family life suffered, including notable challenges for his seven children. Against expectations, Nyerere's children went to government schools, and he insisted they be treated no differently from other students.[51] Being both "normal" children and the heirs of an all-powerful president was not an easy balance for any of them to maintain. Several of his sons joined the military as normal citizens, but a couple of them began to show signs of mental illness, which ran in his family.[52] With Nyerere absorbed in matters of state, the family split up for a while.[53] Maria went to live with her sister in a town near the Kenyan border, tired of living with a husband more married to his country than to her—more the "father of the nation" than of his own children.

In public and in private, however, Maria was ever gracious and ever modest, raising their children according to her husband's austere values. With the humble bearing of a respectable housewife, she ably played the dual role of first lady in diplomatic circles and virtuous mother of the nation for Tanzania's citizens. Her sense of propriety was an invaluable asset in Nyerere's effort to set an example of socialist integrity.

5

Confronting a Continent in Crisis, 1978–90

Ten years after the Arusha Declaration, Tanzania was in the midst of an economic crisis. The country was falling short of almost all the goals set forth in that inspiring speech of 1967. Nyerere had proposed that people, not money, were the key to Tanzania's development. Yet government expenditure as a proportion of gross domestic product (GDP) had increased from 16 percent of GDP in 1967 to 40 percent in 1976. This increase came despite the layoff of nine thousand government workers, a fifth of the civil service. Nevertheless, the country maintained manageable budget deficits at the expense of a heavy tax burden and dependence on foreign aid.[1] An internal report by the Bank of Tanzania warned that declining production across the Tanzanian economy signaled deeper structural problems that could not be explained by recent droughts and oil shocks.[2] The report aimed to disabuse officials of the idea that external events explained internal economic difficulties.

Tanzania's trade balance, which Nyerere considered the key to economic self-reliance, had been in continual deficit since 1969, largely the result of an overvalued shilling. A major goal of the nationalization and villagization policies had been to decrease reliance on imports and increase exports. But imports had tripled since 1967, while exports had only grown by half. The new parastatal industries were inefficient and produced low-quality products. Nationalization of retail trade disrupted supplies of spare parts, clothing, and food. Collective farming had not led to increased production; in fact, just the opposite. Agricultural exports declined throughout the 1970s.[3]

The effect of the stagnant economy and crushing fiscal burden was to make a mockery of the expectations laid out in the Leadership Code. Buffeted by inflation and constant calls for both public and private austerity, an honest civil servant or party official was hard-pressed to maintain a family on a meager salary. Bribery and embezzlement became the norm at every turn. A parliamentary inquiry estimated that losses to the government and parastatals by theft and corruption had increased from ten million to nearly seventy million shillings between 1975 and 1977.[4] The Leadership Code banned political officials from operating private businesses or rental properties, so even these formerly legal means of augmenting a government income were cast as corruption. Rural officials might make the best of it by cultivating a subsistence farm. More highly placed officials did all they could to collect the various perks, allowances, and stipends that probably did more to retard government action than facilitate it. These and other ill-gained funds were often turned into capital for smuggling and backroom deals that flourished in a dysfunctional and overregulated state economy.[5]

Nyerere responded to this crisis as a moralist. For him, the inefficiency and bribery evinced individual weakness rather than bad policy.[6] Surrounded by the prestige and protections of the presidency, he failed to understand the moral dilemmas that people faced as they tried to survive amidst shortages and wildly distorted prices. Because nearly everyone acknowledged his personal integrity, it was hard to challenge him. The few who questioned his authority were pushed aside, cast as traitors, and sometimes imprisoned. Although he had a final say in all detentions, such repression was rarely initiated by Nyerere himself but by an increasingly corrupt political system dedicated to its own self-preservation in his untarnished name.

In early 1978, parliament ministers' decision to grant themselves salary increases and benefits sparked student protests that accused the government of abandoning its socialist principles. In echo of the protest against the national service requirement in 1966, students marched from the university to the State House. Police attacked the marchers, injuring several. Again in echo of 1966, party officials ordered the university to expel 350 protesters, including one of Nyerere's sons, because their actions were "contrary to the national ethic." In the 1966 protest students betrayed a sense of privilege and unwillingness to adhere to socialist values; in 1978 it was just the opposite. The students' accusation that politicians were lining their pockets at the expense of the people resonated in a nation disappointed by policies that had hurt rather than helped their economic condition.[7]

Ujamaa became unsustainable between 1975 and 1980, but Nyerere had invested too much to admit its failure. Droughts, low commodity prices, and oil price spikes were all uncertainties to which markets tended to respond more efficiently than top-heavy bureaucracies. From rural peasants to urban traders, Tanzania's economy had been dominated by petty capitalism for most of its history. Editorial demonizing of rural landholders as "kulaks" and urban businessmen as "parasites" did little to build an alternative economy and only exacerbated racial tensions as Asian traders became convenient scapegoats for deeper problems. Anyone who maintained more than a subsistence income during this period did so by all manner of subterfuge, trying their best to avoid the charge of economic sabotage.

Zanzibar and the Politics of Pan-Africanism

In the mid-1970s the full force of the economic crisis had not yet hit, and Nyerere's power was at its zenith. Even so, many thought that he was preparing to step down from the presidency.[8] Among his peers in other developing countries at the time, he was notably forward-thinking about what his future role should be. Although power blinded him to the negative impacts of his economic policies for average people, he always retained some humility about his position. He insisted on the idea that power lay in the institutions of government and the party, and the president was simply an office-holder on behalf of the people.

In his acceptance speech upon being nominated as the TANU candidate for president in 1975, Nyerere warned against the habit of electing the same person repeatedly for office. "I frequently meditate upon whether it would not be a service to my country if I stood down from national leadership while still in full possession of my senses and strength, in order that I, together with my fellow citizens, could set an example of support and loyalty to my successor. These are not idle or stupid thoughts, especially in a country like ours where the people have known only one man as their President."[9] He offered the term *kung'atuka*, from his home language, which referred to the passing of an older generation from active leadership in the community to the more passive role of elder counsel.

He also proposed that TANU and the Zanzibari ASP should merge, as their independent existence contradicted the idea of a one-party system. Within two years the parties had merged and a new constitution had been written and approved by parliament. The new party, CCM (Chama cha Mapinduzi, or Party of the Revolution), became even more dominant than TANU had been, with the doctrine of party supremacy now written into the constitution.

The merger demonstrated Nyerere's influence and brought him nearly total control of the country through the party structure, but it did not resolve long-standing resentment in Zanzibar about having been bound to Tanzania after the revolution.[10] The Zanzibari public had never voted on the union, nor the merger of the parties, nor the new constitution. The creation of CCM muffled the voices for Zanzibari autonomy, but such sentiment remained strong and began to reemerge after the 1980 elections.[11]

Zanzibari president Aboud Jumbe became a public advocate for the union and a reluctant supporter of the single-party merger.[12] With equal measures of hope and manipulation, Nyerere began to promote Jumbe as his potential successor as president of Tanzania. Jumbe had governed Zanzibar competently since Karume's assassination, improving both its economic situation and human rights record. Putting a Zanzibari in the Tanzanian presidency was another strategy to bind the union more strongly and bring Zanzibaris to identify themselves as Tanzanians. Nyerere had always insisted that the union with Zanzibar stemmed from pan-Africanist sentiment, and this remained his most credible argument.

Pan-Africanism also drove his commitment to the liberation movement, which was gaining momentum. Nyerere continued to be the key voice among the leaders of the Frontline States. He insisted that the final compromise in Rhodesia must allow the creation of a government representative of the majority of the people, and that the new nation could not have multiple armies representing the different African rebel groups and the white national army. It was Nyerere's long-held view that no realistic political solution could ignore "the boys with the guns," namely forces allied with Robert Mugabe and Joshua Nkomo. The new army had to be based on the unified army of the rebel forces, the Patriotic Front.[13] Through a series of stages, Rhodesia became the majority-rule nation of Zimbabwe, and Robert Mugabe won elections in February 1980 to become the country's new prime minister. The emergence of Zimbabwe was a great foreign policy victory for Nyerere, as was the victory in Uganda.

War with Idi Amin

If Tanzania had economic problems, Uganda's were even worse under the corrupt and chaotic rule of Idi Amin. Because of Amin's atrocities, Uganda was increasingly isolated in the world and his government bankrupt, amidst rampant corruption, smuggling, and gangsterism. Facing the threat of a mutiny within his army, Amin created a distraction by claiming that Tanzania was preparing an invasion in the south. Such bluster was not unusual for Amin, who had ordered isolated bombings of Tanzanian cities on multiple occasions in order to intimidate Nyerere. Tanzania hosted thousands of Ugandan refugees and opponents of the regime. Nyerere had also given material support to

Uganda's former president Milton Obote in his initial efforts to overthrow Amin.

Amin began harassing Tanzania almost immediately upon taking power and bombed Kagera Saw Mills in late 1971.[14] Responding to Tanzania's support for a premature invasion by the exiled Obote and his allies, Uganda again bombed Bukoba and Mwanza in 1972. On another occasion the Tanzanian army shot down a Ugandan plane over Bukoba. On October 30, 1978, Ugandan troops invaded Tanzanian territory and occupied a bridge on the Kagera River.[15] The Kagera Salient was a sliver of land between the official border and the Kagera River, which ran just south of the border. It is not clear if Amin ordered the invasion in pursuit of rebels or if it was an accidental spillover from infighting within the army. Whatever the case, Amin used the occasion to claim that Uganda's territory should properly extend to the river and that the Salient was now under Ugandan administration.[16]

In the past, Amin had talked about taking over much larger sections of northern Tanzania. They had all been idle threats before his army took control of the salient. Now his boasted intent "to clean up all the way to Dar es Salaam" had to be taken seriously. A few days after the invasion, Nyerere addressed a large meeting of CCM members in a speech broadcast nationwide. In a soft, reflective voice he summarized Amin's announcement and its implications.

Yesterday he announced that his army has invaded
our country and he has taken the part of Tanzania
that is north of the Kagera River, and that, as of
now, this is part of Uganda and it will be ruled
militarily. . . . This is what he announced himself.
He has helped us by announcing this thing,
because now there is no argument. This is the
situation. What do we do? We have just one task. We
Tanzanians have just one task. It is to hit him. We
have the ability to hit him. We have the reason to
hit him. And we have the will to hit him.[17]

In this understated speech Nyerere provided the
rationale for a full-scale war with Uganda. His stated
aim was merely to force Uganda's withdrawal and
renunciation of the claim to Tanzanian territory. But,
privately, Nyerere made it clear that, in regards to Amin,
his aim was "to get rid of him."[18]

Aside from a handful of troops who had participated in the liberation wars in Mozambique and
Rhodesia, few Tanzanian soldiers had battle experience.
Nonetheless, many Tanzanian officers had excellent
foreign training, and the rank-and-file was well disciplined. Tanzania also called up tens of thousands of
citizen-soldiers who had participated in village militia
training, but these often proved unreliable without close
supervision by career officers. Woefully unprepared for
war, Tanzania slowly built up reliable supply lines for
a large presence in Kagera. On January 21, 1979, three

battalions crossed the Ugandan border and took control of Mutukula, destroying the Ugandan position there. They also leveled the town, killing everyone they encountered, soldier or civilian.

Nyerere was alarmed to hear of the indiscriminate destruction. His unconditional pronouncement to "hit him" was not meant to encourage indiscriminate revenge against all Ugandans. He wanted to remove Amin and, with the counsel of his friend Obote, he hoped for a popular uprising against Amin as his forces advanced. For this, he needed the support of Ugandan civilians. He gave a strict order against harming noncombatants or destroying towns. His officers communicated the order clearly, and Tanzanian troops minimized civilian casualties for the rest of the war.[19] Beyond this order, Nyerere left battlefield tactics to his commanders and concerned himself with politics. He lobbied foreign ambassadors to cut off Amin's oil and weapon supplies and tried to corral the Ugandan exiles into making a plan for the postwar state.[20]

The field commander for the Tanzanian forces was a World War II veteran and Nyerere's childhood friend, David Msuguri, who had once been Idi Amin's instructor. Msuguri had been stationed in Zanzibar, but was transferred to the front to take charge of the invasion. When the commander of the Tanzania People's Defence Force (TPDF), Abdallah Twalipo, died shortly after the war, Msuguri ascended to command of the TPDF.

Tanzania's army faced few setbacks as it took control of Uganda in a cautious advance over the course of several months. Amin's best officers had long ago been killed or sent into exile, and those who remained were of uncertain loyalty. Amin had built up an incoherent mercenary army of demobilized rebels from Southern Sudan and Libyan irregulars loaned to him by Muammar Gaddafi. Ugandan forces lacked a command structure and could do little but take potshots at the advancing Tanzanian troops. Tanzania lost only ninety-three troops to enemy fire while losing nearly twice that many in accidents and friendly-fire incidents.

After the initial occupation of Uganda, Nyerere told an interviewer, "If this was repeated again, I'd go through it. But I hate war more now than I ever did because now I know more about it." He went on to consider the more difficult task of occupying the country in order to rebuild it. "We don't want to get too involved in Uganda because we know they'll end up resenting us. It's an irony that no matter how careful we are, at the end of the day they'll resent our help."[21]

Indeed, many Ugandans thought that Nyerere's goal was to bring his friend Milton Obote back to power. Obote had a strong base of support, especially in his home area in northern Uganda. He also headed what was still the strongest political party in Uganda, modeled in many respects on TANU. But his dictatorial ways late in his administration had alienated much of the Ugandan public. Many of the exiles warned Nyerere that Obote's return would lead the country straight back into crisis. Nyerere took their advice seriously. As

Tanzanian troops approached the Ugandan capital at Kampala, Tanzania sponsored a conference of Ugandan exiles to organize a government that could step in when Amin's forces were defeated. Knowing that Obote would be a divisive presence, Nyerere asked his friend to stay home, which he did. Meeting in Moshi in March 1979, the exiles chose a compromise candidate who was no one's candidate, a bland professor named Yusufu Lule who had hardly been involved in the years of effort to overthrow Amin.[22]

Tanzanian troops took Entebbe and then prepared to march on Kampala. To avoid forcing Amin's demoralized troops into fighting to the death if they were trapped in Kampala, the TPDF left the northern route out of the city open for a Ugandan retreat. Tanzanian authorities communicated with Muammar Gaddafi to pass the message to Amin that he was free to flee.[23] Amin wound up in Saudi Arabia, where his death in 2003 went almost unnoticed. Because of this, TPDF troops and their Ugandan exile auxiliaries encountered little fighting in Kampala.

Victory in Kampala and the occupation of the rest of Uganda went smoothly, but the politics did not. After years of insecurity, fear, and violence, it was almost impossible to build trust. The Tanzanians arranged a hasty inauguration ceremony at the parliament building in Kampala, and Lule was sworn in as president. He was supposed to rule in consultation with the National Consultative Committee (NCC). The NCC represented the various anti-Amin groups, many of whom had been on the ground with the Tanzanian soldiers, including future Ugandan president Yoweri Museveni. Lule quickly alienated the NCC and was pushed out of office. He did not intend to step aside quietly, so Nyerere invited the professor for a state visit in Dar es Salaam and then kept him locked up in the State House for two weeks while the NCC came up with another plan that resulted in a new Ugandan president, Godfrey Binaisa.[24]

Binaisa likewise alienated the NCC within a few months. He was overthrown by a military junta that ruled in consultation with the NCC until elections could be arranged the following year. Nyerere used the threat of withdrawing his troops to encourage cooperation among the Ugandans, but to little avail. Obote returned the following year. His party came out as the big winner in the 1980 elections, and it chose him as their president. Uganda's political scene remained chaotic and the country endured violence and insecurity for years. Nyerere withdrew all troops except a small training contingent, and Uganda entered into a cycle of civil wars that continued until Yoweri Museveni came out on top in 1986.

Economic Collapse

The war in Uganda was estimated to have cost Tanzania 500 million US dollars, and it dealt a death blow to the Tanzanian economy. Nyerere had long tried to limit the import of consumer goods in a doomed effort to reserve his foreign exchange for the materials necessary for economic production: fuel, spare parts, machinery. The war ate up all the foreign exchange he had. Fuel was so short that Nyerere recruited a local Asian businessman to request an emergency allocation of oil from Iran, hoping that the Shi'ite businessman could obtain the favor of revolutionary leader Ayatollah Khomeini.[25]

After the war, an extreme scarcity of consumer goods meant that hoarding and smuggling became common among people of every social class. The informal economy flourished, especially small businesses headed by women seeking to augment meager household incomes: cooking and delivering lunches around bus stops and workplaces, making tie-died clothing, selling fruit and trinkets from homemade stands.[26] But marketing boards were unable to buy and collect crops from the field, and parastatal industries shut down because their factories lacked parts, raw materials, and markets. People remember this period as a time when adults wore burlap sacks and village children had no clothing at all. As a fix, the ruling party pushed for higher agricultural export targets that farmers said were simply unrealistic, given all the constraints placed upon them. Criminality had been on the rise throughout the decade and became even worse with the demobilization of troops after the war. Nyerere's one major asset, people's belief in him as a leader, was under threat as cynicism replaced his idealism.

Desperate for funds, Tanzania began negotiating for debt relief with the International Monetary Fund

(IMF). The pragmatic and experienced minister of finance, Edwin Mtei, led the negotiations. In early 1979, an interim agreement with the IMF provided funds and credit at the price of a small devaluation of the Tanzanian shilling. Mtei still regarded the shilling as woefully overvalued. At official exchange rates the Tanzanian shilling was pegged higher than the Kenyan shilling, even though traders were exchanging one Kenyan shilling for three Tanzanian shillings. Mtei negotiated a deal with the IMF that would open up needed credit in exchange for a two-staged devaluation and various austerity policy reforms, including parastatal restructuring, reductions in defense spending, a wage freeze, loosening price restrictions, raising interest rates, and the relaxation of import controls.

These proposed reforms reflected the influence of the neoliberal "Washington Consensus" at the IMF that withheld loan guarantees until countries accepted the bitter medicine of an economic austerity policy. The reform strategy aimed to minimize government involvement in the economy and represented the rejection of the postwar pattern of activist government involvement in national economies. More specifically, it undermined the socialist model of a state-controlled economy that Tanzania had tried to build.

Mtei presented these proposals to Nyerere, who rejected them out of hand. A visiting IMF negotiator proposed to explain the package to the president personally. Mtei brought him to see Nyerere, who, after listening for a short while, abruptly got up and walked away. Nyerere said the IMF visitors had treated him with disdain and vowed that he would never allow his country to be run from Washington. They should go home, he told Mtei. "I will devalue the shilling over my dead body." Nyerere felt that devaluation effectively stole money from his citizens' pockets to the benefit of foreign investors. Realizing he had reached an impasse with the president, Mtei resigned; some say at the president's request.[27] There were precious few like Mtei who were willing to risk their jobs to give hard advice. If Nyerere was getting bad advice from his advisers, it was in large part because they feared him.

Nyerere stood for the presidency in the 1980 elections despite his earlier reluctance. Many party loyalists encouraged his candidacy, perhaps fearful of facing the crisis that would ensue without him. Nyerere rationalized that "to decline would be to walk away from the front line while the war is going on."[28] He felt that the IMF used its financial resources to impose policies on poor countries to the benefit of wealthy countries, and that its "medicine" was a mask for neocolonialism:

> International action on world economic questions
> has been virtually abandoned, and replaced by the
> use of power and the promotion of nationalist and
> monetarist policy. . . . Africa south of the Sahara will
> pay a total of 12.77 billion USD a year in serving
> just the long-term debt it had accumulated by

1982. . . . These are all transfers from the poor to the rich during a time of crisis. . . . We come back to the terms of trade. The foreign exchange cost of producing sisal goes up with the cost of machines and oil; the foreign exchange earnings of sisal do not go up. Our foreign exchange balance becomes negative, and we cannot afford the spare parts needed to maintain production. . . . Unfortunately, the IMF appears to have a single prescription for every economic ill. . . . It is not surprising that the social price for accepting IMF terms is very often riots, with the police or the army having to be turned on the people. In the case of Tanzania, our one strength is the unity and understanding of our people. If that is destroyed, then we have no base from which to make an economic recovery, much less resume our advance.[29]

Unfortunately, Nyerere's attempts to battle IMF prescriptions through the constriction of imports and coerced export production only exacerbated government coercion. Anybody maintaining a large stock of foreign currency or imported products could be accused of hoarding and detained under the Economic Crimes and Sabotage Act. In practice, the enforcement of this law was often a vehicle for personal vendetta and political control. Officials at all levels saw no recourse other than maintaining some wealth in the form of imported goods.

During this period of economic crisis, a group including military officers opposing the increasingly paranoid one-party state began to plan a coup d'état. The sprawling security system, however, entailing various branches of government and informal networks of informants, made a hostile confrontation with the state nearly impossible. The coup plot was nipped in the bud. Numerous suspects were secretly arrested and a well-regarded ambassador was jailed for several years until it was proved he had been unjustly incriminated.[30] At the highest levels, however, the crisis brought openings for more candid discussion of difficult issues, from economic policy to democratization to the tensions between the mainland and Zanzibar.

Although Nyerere had broken with Edwin Mtei, he had recommended him for one of the rotating posts of director in the IMF. Mtei traveled to Tanzania regularly, now representing the IMF, offering the same advice that had cost him his job. After hearing of Mtei's conversation with the idealistic new prime minister, Edward Sokoine, Nyerere told Mtei, "Edwin, I understand from Edward that you consider that all of us are guilty of hoarding." It was a biting comment, but a signal that Mtei's counsel was beginning to find a sympathetic hearing in Dar es Salaam.

Over the next few years Tanzania instituted a series of emergency economic policies. Initially they were aimed, unrealistically, to push for more production and better management. Eventually they came around to a tentative formula for devaluation and deregulation that more or less followed the advice that the IMF had presented and that Mtei had endorsed in 1979. When the government finally signed a long-term agreement with the IMF in 1986, it could claim it was not a foreign dictate but the result of a five-year process of reform initiated within Tanzania.[31] In reality it had been a five-year process of economic pragmatists finding ways to sideline Nyerere's stubborn insistence on a state-controlled economy, a process only completed after he stepped down from the presidency. But Nyerere's role in retirement was anything but passive.

An Elder Statesman

During this transition from active politics, Nyerere had to face a political culture that regarded his utopian ideals with skepticism if not scorn, and never quite got what he wanted despite his headline-grabbing interventions. As he prepared to retire Nyerere took an active role in choosing his successor. At a party meeting in 1984, Aboud Jumbe's support for proposals to clarify Zanzibar's constitutional identity and autonomy brought Nyerere's wrath. Jumbe had forced out a young lieutenant named Seif Sharif Hamad, who later became a leading Zanzibari opposition politician. Recognizing his political acumen, Nyerere brought Hamad into CCM's Central Committee.

It was Hamad who provided Nyerere the evidence of Jumbe's support for a "three-government" system to replace the awkward compromise that had a government of Tanzania and a government of Zanzibar, with no separate mainland government. Nyerere thought the "three-government" proposal would eventually destroy the union by recreating the institutional basis for separate national identities. Zanzibari motivation may have been as much economic as nationalist, as its foreign exchange earnings from clove exports helped prop up the mainland economy.[32] At a general meeting of the party, Nyerere cornered Jumbe into an unconditional resignation, opening the way for an alternative Zanzibari candidate to rise as the party's choice to succeed Nyerere.

Much internal politicking brought Ali Hassan Mwinyi to the fore as CCM's candidate for the union presidency in 1985. Mwinyi was a Zanzibari Muslim and an experienced civil servant in the union government. He briefly served as president of Zanzibar after Jumbe's ouster. Many claim that Nyerere had supported his young ambassador to the United Nations, Salim Ahmed Salim, but that Salim was rejected by those who saw him merely as a Zanzibari Arab. In reality, Salim's cosmopolitan connections and tastes may have alienated him from the long-suffering bureaucrats in an impoverished country, and the idea that he was loyal to Nyerere's socialist vision made him appear as an obstacle to change. In Salim's defense, Nyerere continued to speak fervently against ethnic loyalties as the basis of politics.[33] The party voted for Mwinyi, and Nyerere supported his candidacy. But once Mwinyi took office, Nyerere became his most vocal critic.

By holding on as chairman of CCM, Nyerere retained a pervasive if weakened hand in Tanzanian politics, offering continuity but also a form of insurance if the political system failed to adapt to a new leader. Nyerere finally stepped down from his party position in 1990. This began a tradition of the outgoing president continuing as party chairman for a period (now less than a year) after stepping down from office.

Despite Nyerere's meddling, Mwinyi pursued his own policies and quickly dismissed several of Nyerere's favorites from his cabinet because they opposed economic liberalization. Mwinyi's opening up of the economy became a period that felt to many like excessive permissiveness. Mwinyi became known as "Mzee Ruksa" (Mr. Permission), in contrast to Nyerere's stringent dominance.

Corruption had been endemic in Tanzanian governance since the 1970s. Mwinyi pursued an anti-corruption campaign, but he could not eliminate the ubiquitous habit of bribery nor the desperate search for economic security in a collapsed economy. Moreover, the process of liberalization was one that by definition violated many of the ethics of governance that Nyerere had continually proclaimed. Devaluation and inflation destroyed the savings of average Tanzanians. The very process of privatizing businesses and allowing the growth of personal fortunes upset vaunted Tanzanian social values, even if those values no longer had much impact on people's lives. Liberalization certainly involved corruption, favoritism, and embezzlement, but it also involved a shift toward competitive business that created legitimate private profits. Witnessing these changes, Nyerere encountered more than just corruption. He watched the rejection and abandonment of his socialist vision.

Abroad, however, Nyerere's reputation was still intact. His voluntary retirement brought him great respect on a continent where leaders tended to cling to office until being forced out by a coup or crisis. His articulate critique of IMF austerity plans resonated in countries across the world that faced the same economic crises in the 1980s and the same impossible choices imposed by IMF demands. In this role, he was selected to chair an international commission to investigate the global economy from the perspective of developing countries categorized as the "global south." The South Commission offered proposals to improve developing economies to better serve their people and their long-term social and environmental sustainability. Working with a future prime minister of India, Manmohan Singh, the task gave Nyerere an outlet for an elder statesman's view of global finance, broad-based development, and economic justice.[34]

An Unquiet Retirement, 1991–99

Stepping down from his chairmanship of CCM in August 1990, Nyerere truly retired from Tanzanian government. But it was not a quiet retirement. He remained extraordinarily active as a vocal public citizen in Tanzania and as a venerated elder statesman abroad. As time passed his reputation was reconstructed and he became a national symbol whose portrait still appears in public establishments next to that of the current president, and whose voice is heard in a daily radio program playing excerpts from his speeches.

His personality had not changed much over the years, nor had his habits. He still attended Catholic mass regularly. He scolded politicians and the public alike in meandering speeches spiced with barbed humor. He returned periodically to his hometown of Butiama to refresh his mind and keep in touch with his agricultural roots. He bore his authority with confidence but a minimum of pomp. He traveled in economy class on his regular journeys abroad. When invited to foreign capitals he requested a small hotel suite for himself and single rooms for his entourage—and demanded price comparisons. Joan Wicken still admonished

Figure 6.1 Retired president Mwalimu Julius Nyerere with his personal secretary, Joan Wicken. © Tanzania Information Services/MAELEZO.

ambassadors and award committees, "We cannot afford expensive hotels and Mwalimu carries his own prestige around with him!"[1] He occasionally cut his journeys short to return for the funeral of a colleague, a relative, or a housekeeper long employed at the State House. He insisted on repaying people for items bought abroad on his behalf. He continued to wear his short-sleeved "Mao" suit and carry a small ebony stick, or *fimbo*, that had been a gift and became an understated symbol of his authority.

Retirement brought him more time in Butiama. He aimed to present himself as a common citizen, but he had always been known as "Mwalimu" and had never really stopped being a teacher. He made a show of playing the retired president who had gone back to farming.

He got up early most mornings and made his way to his fields, where he worked them by hand. When journalists came to visit him, he marched them around his farm wearing a floppy hat and rubber boots. Occasionally they could get him to express some regret about certain policies, like the elimination of the agricultural co-operatives, nationalization of the sisal industry, and his underestimation of the difficulty of central planning. He was even quoted as saying that capitalism had a role to play in Tanzanian development, but insisted that he still believed in the Arusha Declaration.[2]

In the afternoon he might drink a beer on the front porch of the wood-paneled house that the party provided when he retired. He might host a visitor for tea or a bit of wine in the evening. A local Catholic priest recalled stopping by to find the former president playing on the floor with a few of his twenty-six grandchildren.[3] Built on his father's hilltop homestead, the house was ostentatious by village standards, but really no more than what Americans might call a split-level ranch house. In the last year of his life the army completed construction on a fancier house next to the older one. Maria Nyerere now lives in the new house, regularly receiving visitors and schoolchildren who come to visit the museum and mausoleum memorializing her late husband.

The Voice of an Elder

Nyerere hardly withdrew from politics in the 1990s. In speeches, meetings, and quiet lobbying, he still aimed to shape government policy and party ideology. Freed of administrative burdens, he became more willing to question past policy and propose new directions for Tanzanian politics. Nyerere became one among many voices in a cacophonous society bursting free of Ujamaa's ideological constraints and seeking direction for a people unmoored from the purposeful state that Nyerere had built.

The first radical proposal came just before he stepped down from the party, when he advocated an end to the single-party system of government that he had built. Before independence he had proposed single-party government for fifteen years, and, by 1990, the system had been in place for a quarter century. CCM officials had paid close attention to the political and economic changes proposed by Mikhail Gorbachev in the Soviet Union and Deng Xiaoping in China.[4] They watched the fearful dissolution of the European communist world and China's strategic balance between violent suppression of public protest and cautious economic liberalization. Led by Nyerere, who told them, "when you see your friend's head getting shaved, best throw some water on your own," the party decided it was time to reform or face a collapse of authority as had happened in Eastern Europe.[5] The donor countries upon which Tanzania depended also pushed for democratic reform, but it emerged from processes initiated by CCM.

Nyerere felt that CCM had become hidebound and corrupt and that the competition of opposition parties would push it to reestablish grassroots connections with the public. Like two knives rubbed together, he suggested, party competition would sharpen both of them. But, he warned in his last speech as CCM party chairman, "if a multiparty system proves unworkable, the most likely thing to follow it will be either a one person dictatorship, or military rule."[6]

President Mwinyi established a commission under Judge Francis Nyalali to gauge public opinion and provide guidance for reestablishing a multiparty system. The Nyalali Commission surveyed over thirty thousand people, and most said they preferred the single-party system. People feared change. They feared that political competition could turn into ethnic or religious conflict. Perhaps they feared that openly questioning CCM dominance could only lead to trouble with local party officials. Nonetheless, the commission recommended constitutional changes to abolish the single-party state and allow for other political parties, with the provision that new parties could register only if they could show a national base of support and were not vehicles for particular ethnic or religious interests. Lending his authority to President Mwinyi and the Nyalali Commission, Nyerere argued that "we cannot remain an island. We must manage our own change—don't wait to be pushed."[7]

This became a popular reform, even if the new parties could not compete with CCM's national infrastructure and control of the government. The political opening included significant expansion of freedom of speech and many new newspapers sprouted up, bringing alternative perspectives into public debate. In practice, Tanzania remained a one-party state, but a few politicians gave CCM a run for its money.

Edwin Mtei established CHADEMA (Chama cha Demokrasia na Maendeleo, or the Party for Democracy and Development), representing a free-market economic ideology and advocacy for democratic reform. The popular former minister of home affairs, Augustine Mrema, became a powerful candidate for the populist National Convention for Construction and Reform—"Turnaround" (NCCR–Mageuzi). Aboud Jumbe's erstwhile opponent, Seif Sharif Hamad, established the Civic United Front (CUF) in Zanzibar and built up a significant following in the coastal mainland. Although seen as a predominantly Muslim party advocating Zanzibari autonomy, CUF pushed more broadly for human rights and constitutional change to end CCM dominance.

The Nyalali Commission had also recommended changing the United Republic of Tanzania into a "three-government" federation with governments for the mainland and Zanzibar and an overarching federal government. The restructuring proposal stemmed partly from ongoing demands for Zanzibari autonomy, stemming back to the revolution and union in 1964. But it was also a public reaction to the decade of reform since the 1980s. Revising the governmental structure seemed like a logical step to remove the ambiguity in the relationship between the islands and the mainland.

Nyerere energetically opposed the three-government proposal. He saw no evidence as to how the change would improve government. He said a three-government structure was a distraction that would place a greater burden on taxpayers and lead to the breakup of a union that had existed for a generation. He argued that Tanganyika and Zanzibar were both colonial creations that existed as independent states only briefly, and that Tanzania was an authentic creation of independent Africa and the ideal of pan-Africanism.

But the issue never went away. In 1992 the Zanzibari government briefly joined the Organisation of the Islamic Conference (OIC). Initially, the CCM leadership tried to bury the controversial issue, and it was partly Nyerere's opposition that brought it out into the open. Arguing that foreign affairs was a union issue and that Zanzibar did not have standing to join an international organization, CCM blocked the OIC move. But the three-government proposal found mainland support as well. In 1993, fifty-five mainland parliamentarians presented a resolution to establish a separate mainland government.

In 1994 Nyerere published a pamphlet summarizing his opposition to the change. Published toward the end of Mwinyi's second term, the pamphlet was also the beginning of Nyerere's involvement in the selection of the next president. In fact, local observers saw cabinet changes at the time as signs of Nyerere's ongoing influence as "kingmaker." He felt that Mwinyi's passivity had allowed the three-government issue to fester and undermine the presidency, but he insisted on institutional and political processes as the key to orderly presidential succession.[8]

For Nyerere, the key issue was the continuity of the government he had spent his life building. The essential problem was not the Zanzibari quest for more autonomy, but the exploitation of a populist issue that had so little to do with the underlying problems of the economy and Tanzania's place in the world. It was the divisive nature of the debate that most rankled Nyerere's sensibilities. The following year he gave an animated press conference at the Kilimanjaro Hotel in Dar es Salaam that became known as the *nyufa* speech, because of his reference to the "cracks" forming in the edifice of the Tanzanian state—cracks of corruption, separatism, and incipient tribalism. He began by illustrating the dangers of mainland chauvinism as a response to Zanzibari separatism.

> You thought that there is a people who call themselves
> Tanganyikan. There is none. There are Gogo people,
> Nyamwezi people, Sukuma people, Zanaki people,
> Kuria people, Mwera people, so many ethnic groups,
> I can't name them all. You will find that there is no
> single thing called "we the people of Tanganyika." Not
> at all. And as soon as you have committed the sin of

saying "them Zanzibaris," that same sin will eat you up. And I'm going to tell you, may God forgive me for saying this, you'll deserve it. It's impossible to commit such a major sin without punishment. And some punishments are right there in the sin itself, it will come immediately.[9]

These were themes Nyerere had hammered on since before independence: that division was a disease which would spread once the infection started, and that modern African nations were the creations of their own citizens, whose unity had to be a conscious ideological choice. Nyerere's interventions in the 1995 elections came on the heels of the tragic and terrifying genocide in Rwanda in 1994. Nyerere had been observing Rwandan politics since independence.[10] In 1960 he had warned that foreign interests were sponsoring the use of ethnic loyalties in politics, which perpetuated festering violence that finally exploded in 1994. Tutsis were targeted because they were seen as members of the former ruling class seeking a return to power.

In the debates over Zanzibari autonomy and the desire for a separate Tanganyikan government, Nyerere saw signs of scapegoating and separatism of the sort that had fueled civil war and mass killings elsewhere. After all, a similar logic had motivated massacres during the Zanzibari Revolution in 1964, when hundreds, possibly thousands, were killed—mostly members of long-standing Zanzibari families identified with the

Arab upper class that long ago held mainland Africans as slaves. The memory of those events still echoed in debates about the viability of the Tanzanian union and in growing religious tensions. Religious riots in Dar es Salaam and electoral violence in Zanzibar over the next few years seemed to bear out Nyerere's fears.[11] In the meantime, many Muslims saw the union as ongoing evidence of Muslim marginalization, attributable to an alleged Christian agenda secretly pursued by Nyerere since independence.

Given these fears, it was surprising that Nyerere's first direct intervention in the 1995 elections was to support the claims of independent candidates to participate in the upcoming election. The new multiparty constitution required that presidential candidates be members of registered political parties. Nyerere argued that in a multiparty environment, nothing should prevent candidates without a party from campaigning, provided they also had a national base and did not use ethnic or religious loyalty as the basis of their campaign.

The problem was that the independent candidates at the time tended to espouse more extreme positions on these very issues. The Christian ideologue Christopher Mtikila was the main petitioner for independent candidates. A prominent voice for a separate mainland government, Mtikila was the target of Nyerere's sharply worded remarks on mainland autonomy in response to Zanzibari separatism. Zanzibar's former attorney general, Wolfgang Dourado, also advocated the legality of independent candidacy. Dourado had initiated the legal critique of the union's legitimacy in the early 1980s that formed the basis of claims for Zanzibari autonomy.[12]

It would be unusual for Nyerere to advocate a position that countered constitutional provisions for the sake of legal technicalities alone. His intent in supporting this issue is unclear. Perhaps he thought it best to invite more voices into the campaign to spur public discussion. Perhaps he thought the more extreme voices would make moderates look good by comparison. Perhaps he thought that Mtikila's wild-card candidacy would undermine the surging popularity of Augustine Mrema, who Nyerere feared could defeat a CCM candidate.

Nyerere did a lot of backroom lobbying in CCM to eliminate various aspirants for the presidential nomination, and Benjamin Mkapa's eventual selection was widely viewed as Nyerere's doing. The colorless Mkapa was seen as "Mr. Clean" and had long been a loyal foot soldier for CCM in a variety of offices. Nyerere was on hand to launch Mkapa's candidacy and made periodic appearances his behalf.[13] Even so, many doubted whether Mkapa could beat the fiery Mrema. It was an election that brought out members of an older generation that, except for Nyerere, had been nearly forgotten. Oscar Kambona returned from exile for a short run that garnered little attention.[14] A sickly Abdulrahman Babu also returned and briefly considered his own candidacy before throwing his support to Mrema as a counter to

Nyerere on Mkapa's side.[15] In the end, Mkapa won, but there were charges of election fraud in coastal regions. Opposition candidates won in several parliamentary constituencies, including Nyerere's own son Makongoro, who ran as an NCCR-Mageuzi candidate in the Arusha Urban constituency, defeating CHADEMA founder and former finance minister, Edwin Mtei.[16]

In Zanzibar, the CCM candidate, Salmin Amour, won by a dubious sliver, almost certainly the result of vote-rigging.[17] Meanwhile, CUF candidate Seif Sharif Hamad had enthusiastic support, especially in Pemba. Tensions mounted with frustration over the deeply flawed election. Attacks on CUF activists only heightened anger at CCM malfeasance. In a veiled acknowledgement of electoral fraud, Nyerere called for compromise, saying Amour's victory had not been decisive and that he should invite CUF representatives into a unity government. "If he sticks to his guns, then CCM has all the rights to form its government . . . but his doing so would be denying the people of Pemba Island the democratic right to participate in the multi-party system."[18] Nyerere's advice went unheeded.

Prior to the 2000 elections, CCM belatedly began negotiations to create more cooperation with CUF. The agreement brought a relatively tranquil campaign, but more evidence of vote-rigging set off protests after the election. The protests were met with force, and dozens died as police shot live ammunition at demonstrators.[19] Violence and accusations of fraud continued to mar subsequent elections in Zanzibar. In 2013, a presidential commission revisited the issue and proposed a new constitution embracing the three-government structure. CCM politicians scuttled the proposal during revisions, leaving it to die a quiet death, as a scheduled referendum in April 2015 was indefinitely postponed.

The Burundi Peace Negotiations

After the 1995 elections, Nyerere turned his attentions to Burundi, where the United Nations had asked him to step in as a mediator, initially in two sessions in Mwanza in 1996 and in further sessions in Arusha in 1998 and 1999. Horrified by the Rwandan genocide, the international community wanted to contain mounting violence in Burundi, which had much the same the ethnic structure as in Rwanda but where the army had maintained control as a bastion of Tutsi power. Burundi's first democratically elected Hutu president, Melchior Ndadaye, had been assassinated in 1993 and tens of thousands had died in ongoing clashes, with the army maintaining the upper hand. The violence threatened to turn into a bloodbath, as had happened in Rwanda after a Hutu president died when his plane was shot down while returning from peace negotiations in Arusha. Hundreds of thousands were killed in Rwanda as Hutu extremists called on their adherents to kill Tutsis and moderate Hutus, often using the common farm implement, the machete, or *panga*.

American and European representatives wanted to take an active role, as there had been much soul-searching after their inaction in Rwanda. Nyerere invited their counsel but was adamant that resolution in Burundi had to come from a regional initiative. By the same token, he did not want Rwanda to be turned into a laboratory for democratic experimentation that ignored the need for stability and reconstruction. "What Rwanda needs now is considerable time to undertake reconciliation. Should the government accept to be pushed to undertake multi-party elections now, don't be surprised to end up with multi-pangas."[20]

The Rwandan conflict had also sparked a rebellion in Zaire (which subsequently returned to its earlier name, the Democratic Republic of Congo). When western representatives wanted to know more about the spiraling Congolese conflict, Nyerere berated them for their ignorance about their own countries' contribution to the conflict, especially since the United States had funded Mobutu's dictatorship. "You imposed and supported Mobutu for 32 years!" he told them. "We could not do anything. You know how bad Mobutu destroyed the country. This time leave us Africans to try to help Congo. The Congolese people have suffered a lot. Their blood is our blood. Please leave us alone this time."[21] Yet the peace process depended on outside funding, creating tension between Nyerere's desire for a long-term political agreement and donor urgency for more immediate stability.

Facing the military rulers of Burundi in his initial meetings, Nyerere insisted that military solutions

offered "no answer but death. . . . We have to get a political solution." As for the Hutu militias, he tried to put the
conflict in a broader historical context, warning them
away from any meddling by Congolese dictator Joseph
Mobutu, who was still in power at the time. "Politically Mobutu was dying but he was resurrected by the
Rwanda and Burundi crisis. . . . He has no interest in
solving these problems. If I was a friend of [Hutu politician Leonard] Nyangoma, I would have told him that
Mobutu wants to turn him into another [Jonas] Savimbi
[a US-supported rebel in Angola]."[22]

While Tanzania and other regional powers briefly
considered providing a peacekeeping force, Nyerere
sensed this would only escalate the situation.[23] He pressed
instead for economic sanctions as "shock treatment"
to force Burundi's Tutsi-dominated military clique to
the table. Recalling his own stubborn resistance to
economic reform in the 1970s, Nyerere told Burundi's
military leader, Pierre Buyoya, that he was like a finance
minister using IMF pressure to force the Buyoya's government to make tough decisions. As with sanctions
against apartheid South Africa, he said, "they take effect
more slowly than bullets but they work."

With Nyerere refusing to ease sanctions, donors
began to believe rumors that he and regional leaders
sought the elimination of the Tutsi government. Nyerere countered that he expected Buyoya to emerge as
the transitional president (as eventually happened), but
would leave this decision to the Burundians.[24] Citing the

hopeful transition to democracy in South Africa, Nyerere told them that "democracy does not mean that Tutsi are going to be slaughtered. . . . I am quite patient. . . . We must look for a political solution."[25] Nyerere insisted on inclusivity, and participation by even the smallest political groups, but he refused to recognize breakaway factions dominated by their armed wings.[26]

The mediation dragged on for years. American representatives found Nyerere exasperating, while the distrustful Burundian combatants all felt he was favoring their opponents. Burundian military leaders suspected that Nyerere kept the Hutu militias out of the talks so that they could put armed pressure on the Tutsi-dominated military government to negotiate. While this may reflect mere resentment on the part of the military, Nyerere was not naive about the role of armed force in negotiating an equitable peace. Nevertheless, Nyerere insisted on building civilian political institutions as the key to a stable solution. This required a reluctant Burundian military to negotiate with civilian political parties.

Nyerere conducted the Burundian negotiations through the newly formed Mwalimu Nyerere Foundation, which was officially inaugurated in 1996. The foundation was not Nyerere's creation, but he supported the "ka-foundation" (little foundation) in his name, modeled on the Carter Center, if it could advocate for peace, unity, and people-centered development in Africa. It was not an institution to serve as a temple to his memory, nor to promote his particular philosophy, but to promote peaceful progress. As for his own policies, he told the foundation at its launch, "I hope that in studying my 'practices' people will be kind—but also honest. Tanzania can learn from my mistakes as well as from our aims and achievements."[27]

Nyerere oversaw the Burundian mediation until his death in 1999, upon which Nelson Mandela, who had just retired from the South African presidency, took his place. An outsider to the region with unparalleled international prestige, Mandela drafted an agreement and convinced the main parties to sign it. It looked at first like an empty agreement, as conflict continued, but Buyoya surprised many when he stepped down from power in 2003 as agreed.

Ethnic tensions in Tanzania today are almost non-existent, with the exception of ongoing resentment toward Asian minorities, but religious tensions are very real. These stem from ongoing educational disparities between Christians and Muslims, from the dispute over Zanzibari autonomy, and from global political trends that have put down local roots. Yet the government, with significant representation from all religious and ethnic groups, has been dealing proactively with these issues for years. Reflecting on the Arusha Declaration late in his career, Nyerere ignored its economic failure and drew attention to the issues that had always been his central goal: "It is not that peace has come by itself. The source of peace in Tanzania is not that the Arusha Declaration has done away with poverty even a little bit. . . . The Arusha Declaration offered hope. . . . So long as there is this hope you'll continue to have peace. . . . It did not do away with poverty but it has given you all in this hall, capitalists and socialists alike, an opportunity to build a country which holds out a future of hope to the many."[28]

On a hot afternoon in rural Iringa in January 1999, Nyerere made one of his last public speeches. He attended the inauguration of a monument to Chief Mkwawa, who had briefly held his own against the German conquest a hundred years before. Other than a few regional authorities, no other dignitaries were in attendance. It was a crowd of local villagers, a few townspeople, some students, and Maasai herders wandering in from distant homesteads. He spoke on the topic of education, saying that the weapons of Mkwawa's age had been spears, and they were no match for newer technologies. The real weapon of the modern age was knowledge.[29]

In small, unseen events like these, Nyerere's achievement is most palpable. He had been called into national politics by an ethnically mixed group of people from various religious backgrounds. He then gathered, guided, and entrusted a larger group that, despite both sincere and selfish mistakes, built a stable nation in modern Africa. His dictatorial enforcement of "national unity" left behind an entrenched ruling party with a ubiquitous and easily abused police state, but it also created the conditions for the gradual transition to multiparty democracy now well underway. Tanzania is a diverse and sprawling nation with enormous potential for development, but also for division. Scholarship about Nyerere's cozy relations with Catholic authorities has become evidence in the eyes of Muslim observers of religious meddling in politics, while Christians protest proposals to grant government recognition to Islamic *khadhi* courts. Politicians now invoke Ujamaa as a call for more virtuous politics, while businesspeople still harbor bitterness about the harsh and arbitrary effects of nationalization and self-induced scarcity that left the country impoverished. Nyerere's memory is now grist for ideological mills, dubiously evoked by politicians of all stripes, but his own iconoclastic voice still rings forth in books, radio broadcasts, and websites.[30]

Mourning Mwalimu

During the last year of his life, Nyerere knew he was terminally ill, but few outside his family knew how sick he was. Most thought he was going to London for routine medical care in September 1999. On the way to London, his plane stopped in Nairobi and he arranged for the ambassador to Kenya, Mirisho Sarakikya, to come visit him aboard the British Airways jet. He was too weak to disembark. Sarakikya had been the first commander of the Tanzania People's Defence Force and had privately clashed with Nyerere over many issues during their years in public service.

On this occasion, Nyerere just wanted to say goodbye. He told the general that he might not return.

Sarakikya was taken aback and told him not to worry, they had great doctors in England. Nyerere lifted his shirt to show a rash across his belly. "Ni mkanda wa kijeshi," the belt of a soldier, he joked in a whispered voice. "It's leukemia, it's terminal, and it really hurts." At a loss for words, Sarakikya was relieved when the airline attendant alerted him to get off the plane.[31]

At St. Thomas' Hospital in London, Nyerere's wife and children took turns keeping vigil at his bedside. He suffered a stroke in early October and died a week later on October 14, 1999, aged seventy-seven. A requiem mass was held at Westminster Cathedral on October 16. Hundreds from the Tanzanian community in London were in attendance, as well as former colonial civil servants, aid workers, aging hippies, missionaries, and nuns. The Tanzanian high commissioner in London, Dr. Abdul-Kadir Shareef, pointed to the multireligious crowd that had gathered there and gave a solemn tribute "to the passing of a man we love, respect, and admire." The next day, an Air Tanzania plane arrived at the London-Heathrow gate reserved for the British royal family and took the Nyerere family back to Dar es Salaam.[32]

Crowds of mourners flooded the streets of Dar es Salaam as Nyerere's casket was escorted from the airport to his seaside house. Some sang, some wept, some fainted, and others stood in mournful silence. Another requiem mass was held at St. Joseph's Cathedral, where Nyerere had attended mass while in Dar es Salaam. A funeral was held at the National Stadium, attended by throngs of Tanzanian citizens who mingled with minimal separation from the many foreign dignitaries. Hundreds of thousands filed past the body as it lay in state through the night. The next day the coffin was flown to Butiama, where another half-million people had gathered. Uganda and South Africa provided planes to help bring mourners from Dar es Salaam. Mwalimu Nyerere was buried about ten meters from his birthplace.

Graça Machel, the widow of FRELIMO leader Samora Machel, attended the Butiama ceremony on behalf of her new husband, Nelson Mandela, who was traveling abroad. She conveyed her husband's regret, saying he would die of shock if he saw Mwalimu's face in a coffin.[33] With the memories of economic crisis and Cold War conflict fading, accolades from home and abroad were nearly endless. Among the most heartfelt was from his long-serving assistant, Joan Wicken, who told a journalist simply, "He's the finest person I ever knew."[34]

Debates about Nyerere's personal legacy and the impact of his strategies will continue, but there is little doubt that he implemented radical new politics in pursuit of a peaceful, prosperous, and inclusive society. Tanzania's congenial peace today is a testament to his successes. But the price of his stubborn idealism was authoritarian rule that blinded him to the economic dysfunction, secrecy, and cynicism that his policies caused. To invoke his memory, as Tanzanians often do, is to be reminded that politics should be about the passion to make people's lives better while resisting the temptations of power. For this reason, Nyerere continues to serve as a secular icon for the possibilities of politics despite the inevitable limitations of leadership. Even if things did not go as he planned, in Mwalimu Nyerere we meet a leader of rare integrity, intellect, and commitment—and in that sense, a fine person.

Notes

In the interest of brevity, the following notes are intended as a guide to further reading and research rather than a comprehensive list of every source used in writing the narrative.

Chapter 1: Mwalimu Nyerere: A Study in Leadership

1. Deogratias Mushi, "Is Nyerere's Process to Sainthood Timely?" *Guardian* (Dar es Salaam), January 24, 2006, viewed on July 21, 2014 at http://web.archive.org/web/20060509023340/http://www.ippmedia.com/ipp/guardian/2006/01/24/58455.html.

2. Julius K. Nyerere, *Africa Today and Tomorrow* (Dar es Salaam: Mwalimu Nyerere Foundation, 2000), 15.

3. Aboud Jumbe, *The Partner-Ship: Tanganyika-Zanzibar Union: 30 Turbulent Years* (Dar es Salaam: Amana, 1994), 114.

4. Julius Nyerere, speech of March 14, 1995, transcribed and translated by the author from video viewed on June 15, 2015, at https://www.youtube.com/watch?v=jE7oTPXtpas.

5. Julius K. Nyerere, *Our Leadership and the Destiny of Tanzania* (Harare: African Publishing Group, 1995), 17.

6. Julius K. Nyerere, *Freedom and Development* (Nairobi: Oxford University Press, 1973), 84; Abdulrahman Kinana, "The Legacy of Julius Nyerere," viewed on June 15, 2015, at https://www.youtube.com/watch?v=jXEWaGIlf0E.

7. See Frederick Cooper, *Decolonization and African Society: The Labor Question in French and British Africa* (New York: Cambridge University Press, 1996), 1.

8. See John Iliffe, *A Modern History of Tanganyika* (New York: Cambridge University Press, 1979), 40–77.

9. David Livingstone, *The Last Journals of David Livingstone in Central Africa: From 1865 to His Death* (New York: Harper & Brothers, 1875).

10. See John Iliffe, *Africans: The History of a Continent* (Cambridge: Cambridge University Press, 2007), 193–229.

11. Cooper, *Decolonization*, 18–20.

12. Richard Rathbone, *Nkrumah and the Chiefs: The Politics of Chieftaincy in Ghana, 1951–1960* (Athens: Ohio University Press, 2000).

13. W. Scott Thompson, *Ghana's Foreign Policy, 1957–1966: Diplomacy, Ideology, and the New State* (Princeton: Princeton University Press, 1969).

14. Daniel Branch, *Defeating Mau Mau, Creating Kenya: Counterinsurgency, Civil War, and Decolonization* (New York: Cambridge University Press, 2009).

15. Daniel Branch, *Kenya: Between Hope and Despair, 1963–2011* (New Haven, CT: Yale University Press, 2011).

16. Jan Jelmert Jorgensen, *Uganda: A Modern History* (New York: St. Martin's Press, 1981).

Chapter 2: Coming of Age in an African Colony, 1922–53

1. Peter R. Schmidt, *Iron Technology in East Africa: Symbolism, Science, and Archaeology* (Bloomington: Indiana University Press, 1997).

2. Jan Bender Shetler, *Imagining Serengeti: A History of Landscape Memory in Tanzania from Earliest Times to the Present* (Athens: Ohio University Press, 2007).

3. Musoma District Book, 7, Tanzania National Archives, Dar es Salaam (hereafter, TNA); Caroll Houle, interview with author, June 18, 2004, Ossining, NY.

4. Thomas Spear and Richard Waller, eds., *Being Maasai: Ethnicity and Identity in East Africa* (Athens: Ohio University Press, 1993).

5. Shetler, *Imagining Serengeti,* 115–51.

6. John Iliffe, *A Modern History of Tanganyika* (New York: Cambridge University Press, 1979), 240–47.

7. Musoma District Book, 71, TNA.

8. David Msuguri, interview with author, August 19, 2003, Butiama.

9. Joseph Mhunda, interview with author, May 30, 2006, Butiama.

10. Thomas Molony, *Nyerere: The Early Years* (Woodbridge, Suffolk: James Currey, 2014).

11. James Irenge, interview with author, August 20, 2003, Musoma.

12. Molony, *Nyerere,* 176.

13. Julius K. Nyerere, *Uhuru wa Wanawake* (Dar es Salaam: Mwalimu Nyerere Foundation, 2009).

14. Molony, *Nyerere*, 80.

15. Richard Walsh and the Tanganyika Conference of Bishops, *Africans and the Christian Way of Life: Pastoral Letter of the Archbishops, Bishops and Prefects Apostolic to the Catholic People of Tanganyika* (n.p.: Catholic Church in Tanganyika, 1953), 47.

16. James Irenge, interview with author, August 20, 2003, Musoma.

17. Julius Nyerere to Mrs. P. M. Mitford-Barberton, April 22, 1949, CO 981/34, Public Record Office, The National Archives, London (hereafter, PRO).

18. Rev. Kenneth MacKenzie to Alison Truefitt, March 11, 1964, File 4, Shepperson Files, Edinburgh University Archives, Edinburgh (hereafter, EUA).

19. Article on Nyerere, 22–25, File 4, Shepperson Files, EUA.

20. A. M. K. Kalinjuma to George Shepperson, February 16, 1988, File 4, Shepperson Files, EUA.

21. Joan Wicken, "African Contrasts: Report of the Alice Horsman Travelling Fellow, 1956–1957," Somerville College, Oxford, January 1958, 29–36, Papers of Lloyd Swantz, Madison.

22. George Patrick Kunambi, interview with author, August 21, 2004, Dar es Salaam.

23. Julius K. Nyerere, *Freedom and Unity* (Nairobi: Oxford University Press, 1966), 39.

24. William Edgett Smith, *We Must Run While They Walk: A Portrait of Africa's Julius Nyerere* (New York: Random House, 1971), 74.

Chapter 3: TANU and Tanzanian Independence, 1954–64

1. Julius Nyerere to George Shepperson, October 8, 1955, Shepperson File 1, Edinburgh University Archives, Edinburgh.

2. Mohamed Said, *The Life and Times of Abdulwahid Sykes (1924–1968): The Untold Story of the Muslim Struggle against British Colonialism in Tanganyika* (London: Minerva, 1998).

3. Kirilo Japhet and Earle Seaton, *The Meru Land Case* (Nairobi: East African Publishing House, 1967); Rashidi Kawawa, interview with author, August 9, 2006, Songea.

4. John Iliffe, *A Modern History of Tanganyika* (New York: Cambridge University Press, 1979), 512.

5. Ibid., 558.

6. Susan Geiger, *TANU Women: Gender and Culture in the Making of Tanganyikan Nationalism, 1955–1965* (Portsmouth, NH: Heinemann, 1997).

7. Hadija binti Kamba, interview with author, August 1, 2006, Dar es Salaam.

8. Mwanabibi Forodhani, interview with author, August 7, 2006, Songea; Asha Nyonyi Mwarabu, interview with author, August 8, 2006, Songea; Amina Maufi, interview with author, January 2, 2015, Nzega.

9. Iliffe, *Modern History*, 557.

10. Al Hajj Tawaqal Karago, interview with author, September 19, 2006, Kigoma.

11. Julius Nyerere of TANU to Jimmy (T. F. Betts), September 26, 1958, Fabian Colonial Bureau, 121/3 No. 36, Rhodes House, Oxford.

12. Frank Myers, "Harold Macmillan's 'Winds of Change' Speech: A Case Study in the Rhetoric of Policy Change," *Rhetoric & Public Affairs* 3, no. 4 (2000) 555–75.

13. Peter Kisumo, interview with author, June 12, 2006, Moshi.

14. "Sitaki Kutishwa Kwa Migomo," *Ngurumo*, November 20, 1961, 1.

15. William Duggan, DAR to DOS, May 3, 1961, Box 2027, 778.00/5–161, RG 59, National Archives and Records Administration, College Park (hereafter, NARA).

16. Julius K. Nyerere, *Freedom and Unity* (Nairobi: Oxford University Press, 1966), 106.

17. Vedastus Kyaruzi, interview with author, May 21, 2006, Bukoba.

18. N. S. K. Tumbo, "Towards NUTA: The Search for Permanent Unity in Tanganyika's Trade Union Movement," in *Labour in Tanzania* (Dar es Salaam: Tanzania Publishing House, 1977), 13; William H. Friedland, *Vuta Kamba: The Development of Trade Unions in Tanganyika* (Stanford, CA: Hoover Institution Press, 1969).

19. "Tanga Reports of Trade Union Men Quitting TANU," *Tanganyika Standard*, December 22, 1960, extracted in 7B, CO 822/2673, Public Record Office, The National Archives, London (hereafter, PRO).

20. William Duggan, DAR to DOS, October 4, 1960, 778.00/6–360, Box 2027, RG 59, NARA.

21. Nyerere, *Freedom and Unity*, 128.

22. Robert Hennemeyer, DAR to DOS, February 1, 1962, 778.13/1–461, Box 2029, RG 59, NARA.

23. Emma Hunter, *Political Thought and the Public Sphere in Tanzania: Freedom, Democracy and Citizenship in the Era of Decolonization* (Cambridge: Cambridge University Press, 2015).

24. Barrington King, "Results of Tanganyika's Presidential Election," November 14, 1962, 778.00/8–262, Box 2028, RG 59, NARA.

25. William Leonhart, DAR to DOS, December 12, 1962, 778.00/8–262, Box 2028, RG 59, NARA.

26. Paul Bjerk, *Building a Peaceful Nation: Julius Nyerere and the Establishment of Sovereignty in Tanzania, 1960–1964* (Rochester, NY: University of Rochester Press, 2015), 183–94.

27. Christopher Ngaiza, interview with author, May 22, 2006, Kamachumu (Bukoba).

28. Julius Nyerere to John Kennedy, May 16, 1963, and June 18, 1963, NSF Box 124A, Tanganyika 1962–1964, John F. Kennedy Library, Boston.

29. Nyerere, *Freedom and Unity*, 223–26.

30. P. A. Carter, "Note of Talk with Mr. G. Rockey on President Nyerere's Visit to London," August 12, 1963, DO 168/81, PRO.

31. "Rural Settlement Commission Established," press release from Tanganyika Information Services, May 9, 1963, R.20/1.1, 548, Tanzania National Archives, Dar es Salaam (hereafter, TNA).

32. Report of the Africanisation Commission, 1962, EB 18/056.1, 590, TNA.

33. Lt. Col RSN Mans, "Report of Mutiny by 1st Battalion Tang Rifles 20th January 1964," Nairobi, January 22, 1964, Ivan-Smith Papers, CSAS.MF.107–108, Borthwick Institute, York, United Kingdom.

34. Chris Pappas, DAR to DOS, "The Field Marshall John Okello Story," October 3, 1964, SNF Box 2691, POL 15–1 Head of State, Executive Branch, TANZAN 8/1/64, RG 59, NARA.

35. Anthony Clayton, *The Zanzibar Revolution and its Aftermath* (Hamden, CT: Archon, 1981); Michael F. Lofchie, *Zanzibar: Background to Revolution* (Princeton: Princeton University Press, 1965).

36. Jonathan Glassman, *War of Words, War of Stones: Racial Thought and Violence in Colonial Zanzibar* (Bloomington: Indiana University Press, 2011).

37. Julius Nyerere Press Conference, January 23, 1964, DO 226/10, PRO.

38. Timothy H. Parsons, *The 1964 Army Mutinies and the Making of Modern East Africa* (Westport, CT: Praeger, 2003).

39. William Leonhart, DAR to DOS, February 22, 1964, POL 15 TANGAN 1/1/64, Box 2687, RG 59, NARA.

40. William Leonhart, DAR to DOS, April 6, 1964, No. 9a, NSF/CF 103–3, Lyndon Baines Johnson Library, Austin (hereafter, LBJ).

41. Note for Secretary of State, "Zanzibar," DO 213/98, PRO.

42. John Spencer to Richard Nolte, August 18, 1964, POL 15 Government TANZAN, Box 2690, RG 59, NARA.

43. Aboud Jumbe, *The Partner-Ship: Tanganyika-Zanzibar Union: 30 Turbulent Years* (Dar es Salaam: Amana, 1994), 105.

44. DAR to DOS, April 29, 1964, No. 88, NSF/CF 100–4, LBJ.

45. William Leonhart to DOS, September 1, 1964, POL 15–1 TANZAN 8/1/64, Box 2691, RG 59, NARA.

46. Thomas Byrne, DAR to DOS, September 28, 1962, 778.2/10–160, Box 2029, RG 59, NARA.

Chapter 4: Ujamaa and the Race for Self-Reliance, 1965–77

1. Julius K. Nyerere, *Freedom and Unity* (Nairobi: Oxford University Press, 1966), 103–7, 174–75.

2. Henry Bienen, *Tanzania: Party Transformation and Economic Development* (Princeton, NJ: Princeton University Press, 1970), 390–400.

3. Petro Itosi Marealle, *Maisha ya Mchagga hapa duniani na ahera* (Nairobi: English Press, 1947).

4. Nyerere, *Freedom and Unity*, 169.

5. World Bank, *Economic Development of Tanganyika* (London: Oxford University Press, 1961).

6. Barrington King, "Tanganyika Minister of Labour Plans the Use of 'Builders Brigades,'" DAR to DOS, January 6, 1961, 878.02/10–461, Box 2772, RG 59, National Archives and Records Administration, College Park (hereafter, NARA); John M. J. Magotti, *Simba wa vita katika historia ya Tanzania: Rashidi Mfaume Kawawa* (Dar es Salaam: Matai, 2007), 43.

7. Cited in John Carthew, "Life Imitates Art: The Student Expulsion in Dar es Salaam, October 1966, as Dramatic Ritual," *Journal of Modern African Studies* 18, no. 3 (September 1980), 544; also William Edgett Smith, *We Must Run While They Walk: A Portrait of Africa's Julius Nyerere* (New York: Random House, 1971), 30–31.

8. Andrew Ivaska, *Cultured States: Youth, Gender, and Modern Style in 1960s Dar es Salaam* (Durham, NC: Duke University Press, 2011).

9. Taarifa ya Mkutano wa Halmashauri Kuu ya Taifa, March 3, 1965, BMC/11/02/B, 589, Tanzania National Archives, Dar es Salaam (hereafter, TNA).

10. SCCI to Ultramarino, Boletim, "Instabilidade de Nyerere," April 28, 1966, SR 082 9–901, Arquivo Histórico Ultramarino, Lisbon.

11. Background Paper for Visit July 15–16 1963, Briefing Book, NSF 162A, John F. Kennedy Library, Boston.

12. "Prospects for the Tan-Zam Railway," November 8, 1965, 102a, NSF-CF 100.7, Lyndon Baines Johnson Library, Austin (hereafter, LBJ).

13. Jamie Monson, *Africa's Freedom Railway: How a Chinese Development Project Changed Lives and Livelihoods in Tanzania* (Bloomington: Indiana University Press, 2009).

14. Kumbukumbu za Kamati Kuu, December 31, 1966, 12B, BMC/11/04/D, 589, TNA.

15. Julius K. Nyerere, *Freedom and Socialism* (Nairobi: Oxford University Press, 1968), 242; TANU Taarifa ya Mkutano wa Halmashauri Kuu ya Taifa 26–28 Januari 1967," 1, BMC 11/02/D, 589, TNA.

16. Kumbukumbu za Kamati Kuu, June 24 1967, BMC/11/04/E, 589, TNA.

17. This Week in Tanzania, August 4–10, 1967, and July 2–August 3, 1967, POL 2 TANZAN 6/1/67, Box 2513 RG 59, NARA.

18. Oscar S. Kambona, *Tanzania and the Problems of African Unity* (London: TDS, 1968); James R. Brennan, "Julius Rex: Nyerere through the Eyes of His Critics, 1953–2013," *Journal of Eastern African Studies* 8, no. 3 (2014): 459–77.

19. C. T. Hart to B. T. Holmes, "Nzega Cattle Thefts Case," April 25, 1969, FCO 31/432, Public Record Office, The National Archives, London (hereafter, PRO); Joseph Kasella-Bantu, *Tanzanian Voice from Detention* (self-published [1983]), East Africana Collection, University of Dar es Salaam.

20. Frieder Ludwig, *Church and State in Tanzania: Aspects of a Changing Relationship, 1961–1994* (Boston: Brill, 1999).

21. John Ntimbanjayo Millinga, interview with author, August 11, 2006, Peramiho (Songea).

22. Michaela von Freyhold, *Ujamaa Villages in Tanzania: Analysis of a Social Experiment* (London: Heinemann, 1979), 145–46.

23. On the RDA and villagization see Leander Schneider, *Government of Development: Peasants and Politicians in Postcolonial Tanzania* (Bloomington: Indiana University Press, 2014).

24. Interviews by author in Lulanzi village, May 2000.

25. Andrew Coulson, *Tanzania: A Political Economy* (Oxford: Clarendon Press, 1982), 185–201, 235–62.

26. Michael McCall, "Environmental and Agricultural Impacts of Tanzania's Villagization Programme," in *Population and Development Projects in Africa*, ed. John I. Clark, Mustafa Khogali, and Leszek A. Kosinski (Cambridge: Cambridge University Press, 1985), 123–40.

27. Goran Hyden, *Beyond Ujamaa in Tanzania: Underdevelopment and an Uncaptured Peasantry* (Berkeley: University of California Press, 1980).

28. Godfrey Mwakikagile, *Tanzania Under Mwalimu Nyerere: Reflections on an African Statesman* (Dar es Salaam: New Africa Press, 2006), 62.

29. Severine M. Rugumamu, *Lethal Aid: The Illusion of Socialism and Self-Reliance in Tanzania* (Trenton, NJ: Africa World Press, 1997); Sebastian Edwards, *Toxic Aid: Economic Collapse and Recovery in Tanzania* (Oxford: Oxford University Press, 2014).

30. Michael Jennings, *Surrogates of the State: NGOs, Development, and Ujamaa in Tanzania* (Bloomfield, CT: Kumarian Press, 2008); Issa G. Shivji, "Reforming Local Government or Localizing Government Reform," in *The Commemorations of Mwalimu Julius Kambarage Nyerere's 79th and 80th Birth Dates*, ed. Gaudens P. Mpangala, Bismarck U. Mwansasu, and Mohamed O. Maundi (Dar es Salaam: Mwalimu Nyerere Foundation, 2004).

31. Harald Kristian Heggenhougen, "Health Services: Official and Unofficial," in *Tanzania: Crisis and Struggle for Survival*, ed. Jannik Boesen et al. (Uppsala: Scandinavian Institute of African Studies, 1986), 310.

32. Coulson, *Tanzania*, 214–17

33. Julius K. Nyerere, *Freedom and Liberation* (Dar es Salaam: Mwalimu Nyerere Foundation, 2011), 84.

34. Julius Nyerere to Lyndon Johnson, January 2, 1968, 1, NSF/SHSC 52, LBJ; Nyerere, *Freedom and Socialism*, 370–72; Nyerere, *Freedom and Liberation*, 151–54.

35. Jan Jelmert Jorgensen, *Uganda: A Modern History* (New York: St. Martin's Press, 1981), 234–56.

36. "Nyerere: It's Racialism," *Guardian*, August 22, 1972; Ronald Aminzade, *Race, Nation, and Citizenship in Postcolonial Africa: The Case of Tanzania* (New York: Cambridge University Press, 2013), 225–35.

37. "Asians from Uganda Can't Settle Here—Maswanya," *Daily News* (Tanzania), August 10, 1972, 1.

38. Letter from "Disgusted," "Let Them Follow our Example," *Daily News* (Tanzania), April 27, 1972, 9.

39. James R. Brennan, *Taifa: Making Nation and Race in Urban Tanzania* (Athens: Ohio University Press, 2012), 159–95.

40. Christian P. Potholm and Richard A. Fredland, eds., *Integration and Disintegration in East Africa* (Washington, DC: University Press of America, 1980), 150.

41. "Integration by Pressure," *International Herald Tribune*, April 11, 1972.

42. William Leonhart to DOS, May 1, 1965, File 7, NSF/CF 100, LBJ; "Background Note: Mr. Oscar Kambona and His Brothers," East African Dept., February 19, 1969, FCO 31/433, PRO; Saada Meffert, interview with author, July 9, 2013, Zanzibar.

43. B. T. Holmes to East African Department, November 13, 1969, 47, FCO 31/432, PRO.

44. "Zanzibar vs Tanzania: The State of the Union," June 19, 1970, POL 15 TANZAN 1/1/70, Box 2617, RG 59, NARA.

45. David Martin, "Man Who Killed Karume Was Son of an Assassin," *Observer*, April 16, 1972, Whitfield File 5, Borthwick Institute, York, United Kingdom.

46. R. Shaw to P. A. McLean, East African Dept., August 27, 1975, 14, FCO 31/1935, PRO; P. E. Rosling to Mr. Keith, "Human Rights and Foreign Policy," March 1, 1979, 2, FCO 31/2661, PRO; Amnesty International report, "Tanzania 1981," FCO 31/3691, PRO; Ludovick S. Mwijage, *Julius Nyerere: Servant of God or Untarnished Tyrant?* (Leeds, UK: Wisdom House, 2010); "Tanzania," Box 6, Entry UD-06D 27, RG 59, NARA.

47. Hyden, *Beyond Ujamaa*, 156–81; "Taarifa ya Kamati ya Uchunguzi wa Shirika la Nyumba la Taifa," Chama cha Mapinduzi Party Archives, Dodoma.

48. William Leonhart to DOS, November 6, 1965, 49, 7, NSF/CF 100, LBJ; James Spain to DOS, "Nyerere and Rhodesia," September 8, 1977, CREST Database, Carter Library.

49. Henry Kissinger, *Years of Renewal* (New York: Simon and Schuster, 1999), 992, 1016.

50. Quoted in Julius K. Nyerere, *Crusade for Liberation* (Dar es Salaam: Oxford University Press, 1978), 6; Jacqueline Trescott, "Nyerere May Invite U.S. Peace Corps to Return to Tanzania," *Washington Post*, August 11, 1977, viewed at https://www.washingtonpost.com/archive/politics/1977/08/11/nyerere-may-invite-us-peace-corps-to-return-to-tanzania/1eec88ee-965c-4072-b1cb-0c2fc9900dd5/ on September 30, 2016.

51. Madaraka Nyerere, interview with author, June 3, 2006, Musoma.

52. "Nyerere, Julius Kambarage," FCO 31/2875, PRO; David H. Shinn to Alan Hardy, January 4, 1973, ORG 1 Tanzania 1973, Box 4, Entry 5710, RG 59, NARA.

53. DAR to DOS, "Social-Economic-Political Observations on a Trip through Central Tanzania," September 25, 1971, POL 2 TANZAN 1/1/71, Box 2616, RG 59, NARA.

1. J. C. Strong to D. J. Carter, East African Department, "Bank of Tanzania: Economic Operations Report June 1976," April 6, 1977, 25, FCO 31/2142, Public Record Office, The National Archives, London (hereafter, PRO).

2. Beverly Carter, Dar es Salaam, to DOS, "Bank of Tanzania Explores Gaping Cracks in the Tanzanian Economy," April 16, 1975, Reel #P750073–1646—#P750073–1751, Box 73D, Entry 454, RG 59, National Archives and Records Administration, College Park (hereafter, NARA).

3. Andrew Coulson, *Tanzania: A Political Economy* (Oxford: Clarendon Press, 1982), 185–201.

4. Mervyn Brown to M. K. Ewans, "Tanzania Internal," August 8, 1977, 40, FCO 31/2142, PRO.

5. Michael F. Lofchie, *The Political Economy of Tanzania: Decline and Recovery* (Philadelphia: University of Pennsylvania Press, 2014).

6. Julius Nyerere, "The Arusha Declaration: Ten Years Later," *Daily News* (Tanzania), February 8, 1977.

7. Issa G. Shivji, "The Politics of Liberalization in Tanzania: The Crisis of Ideological Hegemony," in *Tanzania and the IMF: The Dynamics of Liberalization,* ed. Horace Campbell and Howard Stein (Boulder, CO: Westview Press, 1992), 43–58.

8. Beverly Carter to DOS, "Nyerere Resignation Rumors Persist," January 30, 1973, POL 15–1, Box 2617, RG 59, NARA.

9. "President Nyerere's Speech on Receiving the Presidential Nomination," September 22, 1975, 21, FCO 31/1935, PRO.

10. J. N. Cumming to P. D. McClean, "The Joint TANU/ASP Electoral Conference," October 1, 1975, 23, FCO 31/1935, PRO.

11. Issa G. Shivji, *Pan-Africanism or Pragmatism? Lessons of the Tanganyika-Zanzibar Union* (Dar es Salaam: Mkuki na Nyota, 2008).

12. "Tanzania Union Is of People—Jumbe," *Daily News* (Tanzania), June 2, 1973, 1.

13. Lusaka to DOS, "Nyerere's Dinner at Lancaster House," September 19, 1979, CREST Database, Carter Library, Atlanta.

14. M. K. Ewans to E. G. Le Tocq, "Tanzania/Uganda," November 17, 1971, 216, FCO 31/1037, PRO.

15. Moon to FCO, "Tanzania/Uganda Border," October 31, 1978, 15, FCO 31/2397, PRO.

16. J. S. Wall to Bryan Cartledge, "Uganda/Tanzania Relations," October 30, 1978, 44, FCO 31/2397, PRO.

17. Transcribed and translated by the author from "Vita vya Kagera (Kagera War)—Part 2 of 4," viewed on June 12, 2015, at https://www.youtube.com/watch?v=HmT8EZJ6hOk. "The will to hit him" could also be translated as "the intention to hit him."

18. Moon to FCO, "Tanzania/Uganda Border," October 31, 1978, 76, FCO 31/2397, PRO.

19. Makongoro Nyerere, interview with author, April 3, 2006, Dar es Salaam.

20. James Spain to DOS, "Uganda Situation," March 10, 1979, CREST Database, Carter Library.

21. For a detailed account of the war with Uganda see Tony Avirgan and Martha Honey, *War in Uganda: The Legacy of Idi Amin* (London: Zed, 1982).

22. Tarsis Kabwegyere, interview with author, May 17, 2006, Kampala; Osiinde Wangor, interview with author, June 9, 2010, Kampala; Yona Kanyumozi, interview with author, June 12, 2010, Kampala.

23. Makongoro Nyerere, interview with author, April 3, 2006, Dar es Salaam.

24. James Spain to DOS, "Uganda: Position of Former President Lule," June 25, 1979, CREST Database, Carter Library.

25. Mustafa Jaffer Sabodo, interview with author, June 7, 2013, Dar es Salaam.

26. Aili Mari Tripp, *Changing the Rules: The Politics of Liberalization and the Urban Informal Economy in Tanzania* (Berkeley: University of California Press, 1997).

27. Edward Mtei, *From Goatherd to Governor: The Autobiography of Edwin Mtei* (Dar es Salaam: Mkuki na Nyota, 2009).

28. "Report on Tanzania—November 1980," FCO 31/2877, PRO.

29. Nyerere, *Freedom and Liberation* (Dar es Salaam: Mwalimu Nyerere Foundation, 2011), 139–43.

30. Ludovick Mwijage, interview with author, July 21, 2013, Hostelbro; Christopher Ngaiza, interview with author, May 22, 2006, Kamachumu (Bukoba).

31. Howard Stein, "Economic Policy and the IMF in Tanzania: Conditionality, Conflict, and Convergence," in *Tanzania and the IMF: The Dynamics of Liberalization*, ed. Horace Campbell and Howard Stein (Boulder, CO: Westview Press, 1992), 59–84.

32. Coulson, *Tanzania*, 199–201.

33. G. Thomas Burgess, *Race, Revolution, and the Struggle for Human Rights in Zanzibar: The Memoirs of Ali Sultan Issa and Seif Sharif Hamad* (Athens: Ohio University Press, 2009), 245–46.

34. South Commission, *The Challenge to the South: Report of the South Commission* (Oxford: Oxford University Press, 1990).

Chapter 6: An Unquiet Retirement, 1991–99

1. Joan Wicken to Ali S. Haji, Paris, August 6, 1992, Safaris and Connected Correspondence 30/12/1992, Chairman South Centre, Mwalimu Nyerere Foundation, Dar es Salaam (hereafter, MNF).

2. Mboneko Munyaga, "Age is Unlikely to Slow Down This East African Elder Statesman and Ex-President," *EastAfrican* (Dar es Salaam), April 14–20, 1997, magazine section.

3. Caroll Houle, interview with author, June 18, 2004, Ossining, NY.

4. Among items under consideration by the party leadership in 1987 was a report by Mikhail Gorbachev, "On Reorganization and the Party's Personnel Policy," January 28, 1987, in Taarifa za Chama cha Mapinduzi, Ofisi ya Mwenyekiti CCM Mwalimu J. K. Nyerere, closed Nov. 1988, MNF.

5. "Nyerere: Kutoka Butiama hadi Butiama," *Raia Mwema* (Dar es Salaam), October 14, 2009.

6. Mustafa Songambele, interview with author, August 8, 2006, Songea; Godfrey Mwakikagile, *Tanzania under Mwalimu Nyerere: Reflections on an African Statesman* (Pretoria: New Africa Press, 2006), 81–92.

7. Dean E. McHenry, Jr., *Limited Choices: The Political Struggle for Socialism in Tanzania* (Boulder, CO: Lynne Rienner, 1994), 64–67.

8. Julius K. Nyerere, *Our Leadership and the Destiny of Tanzania* (Harare: African Publishing Group, 1995), 72.

9. Julius Nyerere's speech of March 14, 1995, transcribed and translated by the author from video viewed on June 15, 2015, at https://www.youtube.com/watch?v=jE7oTPXtpas. See also Henry Muhanika, "Nyerere's Speech Could Set Election Agenda," *EastAfrican* (Dar es Salaam), March 20–26, 1995.

10. "Nyerere Blames Belgium," *Tanganyika Standard*, December 6, 1959, 1.

11. Hamza Mustafa Njozi, *Mwembechai Killings, and the Political Future of Tanzania* (Ottawa: Globalink Communications, 2000); Lawrence E. Y. Mbogoni, *The Cross versus the Crescent: Religion and Politics in Tanzania from the 1890s to the 1990s* (Dar es Salaam: Mkuki na Nyota, 2005).

12. "Nyerere Sparks Off Issue of Independent Candidates," *EastAfrican* (Dar es Salaam), April 24–30, 1995, 18.

13. "Mwalimu Widely Expected to Launch Mkapa's Presidential Bid," *EastAfrican* (Dar es Salaam), August 14–20, 1995, 5.

14. "Presidential Race Shaping Up into 3 Way Battle," *EastAfrican* (Dar es Salaam), July 3–August 6, 1995, 4.

15. Nimi Mweta, "Babu Jets Back to Take On Nyerere in Nationwide Drive," *EastAfrican* (Dar es Salaam), October 9–15, 1995, 7.

16. Bob Karashani, "Unassailable Lead for Ruling Party in Dar Elections," *EastAfrican* (Dar es Salaam), November 6–12, 1995, 4. Edward Mtei, *From Goatherd to Governor: The Autobiography of Edwin Mtei* (Dar es Salaam: Mkuki na Nyota, 2009), 202–5.

17. Mohammed Ali Bakari, *The Democratisation Process in Zanzibar: A Retarded Transition* (Hamburg: Institut für Afrika-Kunde, 2001), 209–50.

18. Quoted in "Persecution Fears Mounting after Zanzibar Election," *EastAfrican* (Dar es Salaam), November 6–12, 1995, 5.

19. Ben Rawlence, "Briefing: The Zanzibar Election," *African Affairs* 104, no. 416 (July 2005), 515–23.

20. "Important Pronouncements on the Great Lakes by Mwalimu Julius Kambarage Nyerere," Documents on Burundi Peace Talks, 1996, Burundi Peace Talks, MNF.

21. Ibid.

22. "Audience with Defence Minister at Source du Nil Hotel—Bujumbura," May 21, 1996, Mwl. Nyerere's Discussions/Interviews with Rwandese/Burundian Leaders and Miscellaneous Documents, Burundi Peace Talks, MNF.

23. "The Current Situation in Burundi and Tanzania's Options," Documents on Burundi Peace Talks, 1996, Burundi Peace Talks, MNF.

24. Howard Wolpe, *Making Peace after Genocide: Anatomy of the Burundi Process* (Washington, DC: United States Institute of Peace, 2011), 14.

25. "Audience with Defence Minister," Bujumbura, May 21, 1996, MNF.

26. Kristina A. Bentley and Roger Southhall, *An African Peace Process: Mandela, South Africa, and Burundi* (Cape Town: HSRC Press, 2005), 63–69.

27. Julius K. Nyerere, *Africa Today and Tomorrow* (Dar es Salaam: Mwalimu Nyerere Foundation, 2000), 24.

28. Quoted in Issa G. Shivji, "Critical Elements of a New Democratic Consensus in Africa," in *Reflections on Leadership in Africa: Forty Years after Independence*, ed. Haroub Othman (Brussels: VUB University Press, 2000), 35–36.

29. Julius Nyerere, speech, January 1, 1999, "Sherehe za Uzinduzi wa Mnara wa Kumbukumbu ya Miaka 100 ya Kifo cha Mtwa Mkwawa Huko Mlambalasi Kalenga-Iringa Tarehe 04–01–1999," audio tape in author's possession.

30. See John C. Sivalon, "Roman Catholicism and the Defining of Tanzanian Socialism, 1953–1985" (PhD diss., University of St. Michael's College, Toronto, 1990). Also Marie-Aude Fouere, *Remembering Julius Nyerere in Tanzania: History, Memory, Legacy* (Dar es Salaam: Mkuki wa Nyota, 2015); Chambi Chachage and Annar Cassam, eds., *Africa's Liberation: The Legacy of Nyerere* (Nairobi: Pambazuka Press, 2010); Hamza Njozi, *Muslims and the State in Tanzania* (Dar es Salaam: Dar-es-Salaam University Muslims Trusteeship, 2003); Thomas J. Ndaluka, *Religious Discourse, Social Cohesion and Conflict: Muslim-Christian Relations in Tanzania* (Zurich: Lit Verlag, 2012); Pius Msekwa, *Reflections on Tanzania's First Multi-Party Parliament, 1995–2000* (Dar es Salaam: Dar es Salaam University Press, 2000); Max Mmuya, *Tanzania: Political Reform in Eclipse* (Dar es Salaam: Friedrich Ebert Stiftung, 1998); Jonas Ewald, *Challenges for the Democratisation Process in Tanzania: Moving Towards Consolidation 50 Years after Independence?* (Dar es Salaam: Mkuki na Nyota, 2011).

31. Mirisho Sarakikya, interview with author, June 10, 2013, Arusha.

32. "Tanzanian Press Coverage of Mwalimu's Death," *Tanzanian Affairs*, no. 65, January 1, 2000.

33. Murray Oliver, "Mandela to Visit Nyerere's Grave," *Monitor* (Kampala), October 24, 1999.

34. Joe Khamisi, "Thousands Attend Memorial Service," *Independent Online*, October 19, 1999, viewed on June 14, 2015, at http://www.iol.co.za/news/africa/thousands-attend-memorial-service-1.16701?ot=inmsa.ArticlePrintPageLayout.ot.

Index

163

CPSIA information can be obtained
at www.ICGtesting.com
Printed in the USA
FFHW021055011218
49684491-54069FF